'*Where did that voice come from*, asks one of the voices here, *that was telling me I wasn't doing anything right?* This is one of the serious questions *Pretenders* investigates, together with the ways in which our sense of self is pressure-formed by the roles we perform and are expected to perform. The voices worry about neediness (like you, like me), but their project is thoroughly generous: here are individuals feeling along the paradoxes of pretence and the precarities of selfhood for our collective benefit. Their disclosures, and the author's own, rhyme with Potts' (characteristically sharp-eyed) excursions into historical imposture; the result is a hall of mirrors in which readers may see themselves and others reflected a bit more clearly, a bit more kindly. If you've ever had the feeling that you're *not good enough*, you should read this book. If you've never had that feeling, then you must read this book.' – ABIGAIL PARRY

'With the intimate air of a secret vouchsafed, *Pretenders* is an immersive, compelling, original work of documentary poetics. Potts takes on the role of poet as filmmaker, cutting between voices: we feel her guiding presence behind each frame, and her skill. Across the collection's trans-membered testimonies, lyric tension creeps back in via the poems' consummate rendering of hesitation, emotion, and silence on the page.

As a study of imposter feelings, *Pretenders* is revelatory: humane in its ability to hold and make space for vulnerability, and alert to the socio-political dynamics that underpin the impulse to self-doubt. Whatever mode she's working in, Potts is an essential poet.' – SARAH HOWE

Kate Potts is a poet, academic, mentor and editor. Her second collection, *Feral* (Bloodaxe Books, 2018) was a Poetry Book Society Recommendation and a *Telegraph* poetry book of the month. Her debut pamphlet *Whichever Music* (tall-lighthouse, 2008) was a Poetry Book Society Pamphlet Choice and was shortlisted for a Michael Marks Award. Her first full-length collection was *Pure Hustle* (Bloodaxe Books, 2011). Her third, *Pretenders*, was published by Bloodaxe in 2025.

Kate writes about creative writing and everyday life, including the intersections and tensions between writing and caregiving, in her newsletter *Speak Up! On Writing, Failing Better, and Taking up Space.* She lives in Stroud, Gloucestershire, with her son.

KATE POTTS

PRETENDERS

BLOODAXE BOOKS

ISBN: 978 1 78037 730 8

First published 2025 by
Bloodaxe Books Ltd,
Eastburn,
South Park,
Hexham,
Northumberland NE46 1BS.

www.bloodaxebooks.com
For further information about Bloodaxe titles
please visit our website and join our mailing list
or write to the above address for a catalogue.

Supported using public funding by
**ARTS COUNCIL
ENGLAND**

Cover design: Neil Astley & Pamela Robertson-Pearce.

Printed in Great Britain by Bell & Bain Limited, Glasgow, Scotland, on
acid-free paper sourced from mills with FSC chain of custody certification.

For Jude

ACKNOWLEDGEMENTS

Thanks to the editors of the following publications in which some of this work first appeared: *The Moth, Mslexia, Notes from the Edge: Dialect Writers Anthology 2023, The Poetry Review, The Sociological Review*, and *The Telegraph*.

A previous version of 'A Telephone Conversation with My Sister/Footnotes' was shortlisted for The Moth International Poetry Prize (2020). 'Bloom' was highly commended in the Mslexia Poetry Competition (2019). 'Past Tense' is included in Poetry By Heart's *14+ Timeline Anthology*. 'Lullaby No. 3' was commissioned for the event Future Karaoke #3: The Cambridge Book of Magic (2023).

A huge thank you to Neil Astley and Alison Winch for encouraging and enabling me to speak as an author in this book, rather than hiding. For poetry inspiration, feedback and unfailing support, thanks to Alison Winch, Holly Hopkins, Angela Cleland, Jon Stone and Cath Drake. Thanks also to Mimi Khalvati for her astute editing suggestions, to Kayo Chingonyi and S.K. Perry for believing in and encouraging this project in its early stages, and to Generative Constraints for helping me to think productively about multi-vocality. Thank you to my sisters, Ruth and Ellen Potts, for conversations and advice. Lastly, thank you to my interviewees: Tiffany Anne Tondut, Peter Ormerod, Lolita Parekh, S.A. MacLeod, Lynn, Tabitha, Sinéad, Olivia, Michelle, Jacob and Eve, for your kindness, enthusiasm, and candour.

I am very grateful to Arts Council England for an award towards the writing of this book.

CONTENTS

9   Introduction: Among the Pretenders
14   The Real Bird

17   *Dwellings:* voices

33   A Telephone Conversation with My Sister/Footnotes
37   Imposters (1). Grand Duchess Anastasia of Russia
     (Anna Anderson/ Franziska Schanzkowska)
38   Dwellings

41   *Work, Work, Work:* voices

71   Coping with Redundancy
73   Imposters (2). James Gray (Hannah Snell)
75   Imposters (3). Anna Delvey (Anna Sorokin)
77   Shipwreck/ The Iron Lady

79   *Bodies/Care:* voices

95   Imposters (4). Princess Caraboo (Mary Willcocks)
97   Bloom
98   Conception

99   *Rites/Resolutions:* voices

120   Past Tense
122   Lullaby no. 3
123   After Pretence

127   NOTES

Introduction: Among the Pretenders

The term 'The imposter phenomenon' first appeared in Pauline Clance and Suzanne Imes's paper 'The Imposter Phenomenon in High-Achieving Women', published in the year of my birth, 1978, towards the end of second-wave feminism. Women's failure to believe in their own success was, the writers suggested, partly a result of internalised stereotypes: 'If she were to acknowledge her own intelligence, she would have to go against the views perpetuated by a whole society – an ominous venture indeed!' To avoid acknowledging and enjoying authority and achievement could be, Clance and Imes argued, an unconscious protection against disapproval and attack. There were also, they concluded, other factors – such as particular behaviours and configurations in family relationships – that made some women prone to imposter feelings. Later studies have found that men also feel like frauds, though being part of a group which is negatively stereotyped, for example according to gender, class or ethnicity, can make experiencing the imposter phenomenon more likely.

At the beginning of the 21st century, particularly in workplaces, the narrative shifted away from Clance and Imes' 'imposter phenomenon' and towards 'imposter syndrome', an internal barrier to success that could be overcome through classes, coaching, self-help books, and positive thinking. Ruchika Tulchyan and Jodi Ann Burey's 'Stop Telling Women They Have Imposter Syndrome', published in *Harvard Business Review* in 2021, was part of a backlash against this, determined to shift the focus back towards hierarchy, power dynamics and prejudice. Tulchyan and Burey argued that 'Imposter syndrome is especially prevalent in biased, toxic cultures that value individualism and overwork.' In 'Am I an Imposter, Or Am I Oppressed?' (2017) Shivani Seth also challenged this more individualistic approach: 'Those [imposter] feelings didn't come from some magic place that could be addressed by a back-to-school special and a hug. They came from racism, queerphobia and white supremacy.' Recently, use of the term 'imposter syndrome' has exploded, to the point where it begins to seem too general, simplistic or blunt to be useful. Research suggests that up to 80% of us are likely to feel like imposters at some point in our lives. Leslie Jamison, writing in *The New Yorker* in 2023, argued instead for careful use of 'the imposter phenomenon', a label that suggests a complex experience influenced by multiple factors rather than a diagnosis.

Writing about her experience as a feminist academic for the *Sociological Review* magazine in 2017, Maddie Breeze said: 'Failing to meet some definitions of success – publicly, collectively, and strategically – might expose how feeling inadequate and inauthentic is a function of assessment according to criteria that not only are impossible to meet, but that one wishes to reject...' When I first read Breeze's article, it subtly but profoundly rearranged the furniture in my mind. I was a poet and early-career academic in my early 40s, and I badly wanted to be a parent. I was trying to navigate short-term and zero-hours contracts and a high-pressure, long hours work culture, along with queasy levels of global political and economic volatility. Breeze's ideas around imposter feelings chime with British psychoanalyst Donald Winnicott's theory that imposter feelings can point to a tension between the external 'False Self' and our true needs and desires. Could imposter feelings, in some cases, be a warning against unhealthy compliance, a bad fit between person and environment, a rift between who we think we are, or should be, and what we really need? Feelings of fraudulence might, in some cases, be a signal that things need to change.

What if, rather than shutting imposter feelings away or overriding them, we were to bring them out into the open and have honest conversations about them?

From the very beginning my sense of myself as an existing,

legitimate being has been developed in relation to others: the ways in which I've been seen, acknowledged, and allowed to take up space. I think the imposter phenomenon and the thinking and emotions that create and sustain it are woven – or maybe welded – into the fabric of our histories, our social and cultural structures and processes, and our interpersonal relationships. The power and value systems that produce and reproduce, for example, class, race, gender, or national identity, are also an integral part of our family dynamics, and of how we learn to experience, know and value our selves.

'We all feel like imposters, don't we,' people often say. It's true that most of us do. But collapsing experience into sameness risks overlooking huge differences in lived experience: one person might feel an uneasy sense of fraudulence in a single job interview; another might feel like an undeserving fraud in ways that permeate their entire life.

The kind of discomfort I'm describing here, and the seeming irrationality of imposter feelings, tends to lead us to want to feel in control when discussing them. We want statistics, arguments, conclusions, affirmations, ten positive steps we can take to fix the problem right now. What we risk losing is a genuine, curious exploration of personal and bodily experiences of imposter feelings – as well as the surprises and insights this might create. It can be hard to apprehend the messy, often maddeningly frustrating experience of feeling like a fake. Through this book, I wanted to prise open those spaces of discomfort through poetry and through conversation, letting silence and uncertainty spill onto the page rather than rushing too quickly to draw conclusions or shape a narrative. Through my own poems and interventions, I've attempted to enter into a different mode of dialogue to and with the interview texts, peering at imposter feelings via my own narrative of exploration and discovery. In my poems about historical imposters, I wanted to examine actual pretence and fraudulence – its freedoms, terrors, and contradictions – as a sort of counterpoint or photographic negative of imposter feelings.

My work on this book was sparked off by Maddie Breeze's work on 'Imposter Syndrome as a Public Feeling'. I've also been inspired by the BBC's 'actuality' radio feature documentaries of the mid 20th century, and by multi-voice works for the page like Svetlana Alexievich's *Second-Hand Time*.

The interviewee monologues in this book are constructed from live interviews and conversations conducted in person, on the phone and over Zoom. I found participants for the project via a series of callouts. Although I tried hard to reach beyond my own networks, and to include people with very different lives from mine, I found that the people who responded tended to be those that already knew me or knew of me, and who worked in the arts, education, or caring professions. Perhaps this is because talking about imposter feelings requires a certain level of trust. It can also require, as interviewee Tabitha points out, a certain degree of privilege.

As far as possible, I tried to ask all interviewees the same 10 questions. I edited the transcripts for clarity, structure, form and rhythm, but I have tried hard to maintain and stay true to the essence of each person's statements. I've also attempted to capture, on the page, the rhythms and particularities of the bodily voice and breath, a sense of the person as existing in the space beyond the page. I've done this through gaps, absences and silences, and through the shape of the text. Sometimes I've added sensory detail that seemed present in the actual conversation but not in the recording of it. With many of the interviewees, I've asked for extra detail or clarification, and the work has become a continuing collaboration. For all of the pieces, I have checked the work in progress with participants to make sure they're happy with it, and I've made changes as requested. I understand the importance of respecting these voices and their integrity, as far as possible. I hope this work – this collection of voices – functions as something generative, a starting point for new conversations.

KATE POTTS

The Real Bird

Not a Sunday-pink pedalo
with a fibreglass, arching neck.

Not a fairground mannequin: glued-on
nylon feathers, mechanical pistons and glass eye.

Not a cursed, enchanted human daughter
with sorry beak and pinned wings

or a brutal god in disguise,
or a ballerina: taffeta, razor's edge, wire.

Not one for sorrow, two for joy; no
flapping omen or ghoul; not a human ghost

migrating from the underworld; no pecking swarm
that blots the sun; not siege, nor charm

but bird: bold and tall on the reservoir path.
There's something you want to say.

You lift a webbed foot to scratch
your oxters, your waxy feathers.

Not a honk, quack, grate, or rattle. More like
cricket's wings in the dusk, staccato;

a blue, repeated call. I am trying
to listen, listen, listen.

DWELLINGS

voices

Lynn

I never actually expected you to call me, so…
Here we are.
Do you want the video on or off?

The first time I felt like an imposter?

It was going to somebody's house who was in my class
at school.   She and I were quite good friends.
We sat beside each other at school and played together a lot.

So I went there   and I was amazed
   by their house,   much bigger and posher than ours.
She and her brother had their own bedrooms,   up big stairs,
a front room with French windows to a back garden…
                        It was not what I had.   But I didn't
realise. Well of course I realised.   That I didn't have
what she had. But I'd never   really looked at anything
before quite in those terms. It was an eye-opening situation.
About where we come from.   Where I come from.
And where she came from was different.

I thought, 'Oh they've invited me here but they don't know
where I'm from.'

                        Of course, this is very many indeed years later.

I've realised how much it has to do with other people.
         You know?   Other people
and the situations that you're in.   It doesn't just come
in inverted commas: 'I feel like an imposter.'   It's much
bigger than that, and the contextualisation is really important.

My mother had to walk me around the streets rather than
breastfeeding on demand.

That was the childcare wisdom at the time…
Deprivation.   Deprivation might well come from there,
        rather than
not having your own bedroom,   sharing with your sister.
                            We can afford to feel sorry for boys
who were educated at Eton.   They were deprived
in a different way to those who were brought up   in a home
with little space.

For me it's a feeling of inferiority.   Even though
I know I'm not inferior. It's always   that relational
thing. You know. Inferior to – what? Inferior to – who? –
and why?

I felt much more comfortable among people   who lived
in the same kind of housing that I did.   Or, I felt
much more at home with people who didn't belong.
You know? From Poland and Ukraine.   Or who had been
born here, but whose parents were African.
There was something about them,   I don't know,
that wasn't fixed.   That wasn't ingrained and blind.

I've never used those words before   but that's how it was.

Author

I do the first exploratory interview on zoom while breastfeeding my son, who is a few months old.

It's a sunny, funny chat, the woman pulling pink faces on the screen to entertain my baby. When Í sent her the interview text, though, she feels exposed.

'Did I say that?'

She doesn't want to be identifiable. She's worried about what people might think, how readers will respond. A lot gets lost between live conversation and the page, so I add some small, concrete details to try to ground the discussion a little more in physical reality. But these additions sound like my voice. Is this my text, or hers?

Michelle

I suppose it's the family culture: *Don't show off. Children should be seen and not heard.* On the bus, my pa would take off his cap – submissive.

My parents behave like this when they go out. Deferential: doctors are amazing –

   famous people are always amazing.

I remember when I went to university,   I didn't understand
 how all the words and systems worked.

My friend Gabby – her parents were doctors – she was a real student and I was just tagging along.
I always felt that she would know best in all situations there.

I don't agree with hierarchies.   I believe
that everyone is of equal value. So why do I feel inferior?

I'm questioning if I actually have imposter syndrome now;
it depends on the context.   Sometimes you feel like
an imposter and sometimes you think
        Of course I belong here.

Fingers crossed your baby will be OK while we're talking.
I can keep making funny faces to entertain him.   I could
put the elephant on my head…

At school the people who were good at English always
seemed to be a bit posh.

I remember being a child and playing with people in that
direction and thinking,   you know, maybe
I should be playing with those people in the other direction.
Scuzzy knees. Knock down Ginger…
                        Some of my friends from my hometown
are actually quite middle-class, for my hometown.

When I was a teenager we used to go to this club, Weekends
at The Brewery. It was all the gothy people, LGBTQ people,
people of colour (there were only two people of colour in my
hometown,   but they were both there). Basically,
all the people who didn't fit in.

I think it's also to do with culture, with subculture.
    You discover books and films and you don't want to dress
like everyone else. You start wearing funny clothes – leather
and fishnets – paint your face like a ghost and backcomb
    your hair.

You go out dancing. It could make you quite snobby about
'mainstream' culture.

Peter

There's a difference between feeling out of place and feeling
     unqualified; it's an interesting flip between the two.

You go from thinking   'Why am I here with these people?'
     to 'Oh my goodness, I'm going to get found out.'

It's quite a subtle thing but you can start humiliating
     yourself fairly easily and start feeling –   feeling
     small and, yeah,   it's a curious sort of, curious,
          curious   sense.

I can hear you, yes. Are you outside? It's a bit windy. That's
     better now. Where are you walking?

I remember going to a swimming lesson…
I remember going to a swimming lesson. I think I was
     four years old   when I was living in Swindon.

I remember the turquoise and white checked tiles.
     Echoing and screaming, and lots of kids standing
     in a row. And the assumption was from the teacher
     that all the kids knew how to swim. And I had no idea
what I was doing.   I remember thinking *Oh my
goodness. The teacher thinks that I can do stuff that I can't.
     This is a horrible feeling.*

And of course, in a swimming pool it's literally sink
     or swim.   If you can't swim, you can't swim.

     There was no way I could fake it.
     I remember that feeling very strongly. I didn't think
in these words, but: *I'm obviously here under false pretences.*

I had a really mixed, sort of, childhood. I might have
        mentioned this in the questionnaire. Sort of this
mixture of
        growing up in a sort of very middle-class family who
        do lots of reading and, you know, middle-class
        cultural pursuits
but living in a really rough council estate. And in primary
        school, all my friends were estate kids. I really liked
        that. But it led to this sense perpetually that...
Among my school friends I obviously stood out a lot.
Among my parents' friends I stood out a lot.

Tiffany

We lost everything. My father
went back to Australia. So I developed, sort of, *daddy
        problems*. And there were class issues, going from
a middle-class house – Rose Cottage, cream with latticed
windows – and moving into the tiny terraced house
        on Cowper Road, having been evicted. I mean, it was really
traumatic stuff.

    I had a sky room with a ladder,
        I could look at the stars. But my father's room
was dreadful.   It still haunts me: the sick-green
walls and the box bed he slept on. It was   too short.

    I could see this from the landing, his long legs
over the edge. And he was smoking – the green and the
        smoke and the too-long legs. I realised what we'd lost.

    But d'you know what? The word *illusion* comes
        into my mind now. I remember talking about this
with one therapist, and my borderline personality disorder...

My father was a great storyteller.　　　He was a great man
in many respects. He made　his own money – sales,
property development – made his own business. He came
from nothing. He made up stories all the time, he loved
　　　to exaggerate.

　　　　He could spin a story on the spot,
　　　often embellished anecdotes. He once told hosts
that I could 'play everything from Mozart to Beethoven' on
the piano, which wasn't true. He was proud of me
　　playing a tune for them.

He invested in Armani suits and ties, accessories…
　　to give the illusion to investors that he was
still prosperous.

　　　He'd had a difficult relationship with his father.
That's why he was building his empire. It definitely
rubbed off on me
　　from a really early age.
　It came down to me; I inherited something through him.

　We all live in a state of psychological conflict to varying
　　　degrees. People need to have a sense　　　of self-
worth instilled in them; they should grow up with that
　　　　as a solid inner core.　　Sorry –

　　can you repeat the question?

We all need certain levels of love　and acceptance. We all
need praise and constructive criticism. Otherwise, the lack…

It's that vulture or monster that perches on the end
　　of the bed.

Olivia

Sometimes – it's ridiculous – I've got a really lovely group of
friends – sometimes I'm like, *Am I really part of*
   this group? I have to rationalise it again and say
   No, I've been friends with these people for 10 years.
         It's a feeling of not belonging.

Losing my father was a big thing. And then being
a perfectionist. I think as a child I used grades or doing well
at school as my self-worth.   And then when you get older
and you start a degree   it's not so easy and then you feel,
       Oh, I'm not achieving.

So the boundaries change.

Eve

My grandfather was a real stickler, he was strict.
A real patriarch. My mum really looked up to him
   and so did the rest   of the family.
And, you know, if you had the approval of grandfather
then you were a kind of shining cherub…   So I think
that's the root of it for me.

When I grew up my brother, who's much cleverer than me
I always think… He's really sharp, witty and bright…
he went completely off the rails as a teenager.
And then I think there was an expectation on me
   to not go off the rails,
     to make up for the things that he didn't do.

There's definitely some stuff about being 'a good girl'.
I've done a lot now, especially recently, to try… to try
to not let those expectations burden me. I can be

quite a people pleaser. I have to be quite careful sometimes
    because it burns me out.   You can't drink
from an empty well.

My mum gave me for my birthday this year – it was quite
tongue in cheek – but she gave me this massive badge
that said, 'Wonder Woman'.

She gave it to me,   and the next day I found out
I had covid.   And I was trying to run an artist's retreat
online, trying to go hybrid because I didn't want
to let all these people down who'd taken a week off work.

And I was just looking at that bloody badge and just thinking
– which is partly why my mum gave it to me, I think.
    It's such a poisoned chalice.   Just, you know….
I just want to chuck that badge out of the window.

Author

I work on the Arts Council funding application for
Pretenders at my sister's house with a sweet-smelling,
damp, napping baby on my chest. It's my second try
for the funding.

When I get the email and log into the portal to find
I've been awarded the money, it's an extraordinary,
shining relief, like a laser beam of light through fresco
clouds. I yelp, and jump up and down on the spot. *I can
do this*, I think. I can be a solo parent and still write.
I'm not desperate, or abject, or bitter. My career/ love
life/ potential aren't over. Though I am bitten, gnawed
and frayed, changed in irrevocable and unexpected
ways.

Tabitha

I'm very fortunate in that I've had a very supportive family,
        great friends. I've not really had to worry
about money growing up.   I'm sure all this has helped.
    Although I have friends who've had all these privileges,
but still don't have that same sense of agency or control.

I don't know where that comes from…
It would be great to speak to a psychologist, somebody who
could shed light on that…

The chief executive of a health charity –   on the first day
    that he started in that role he tweeted something about
his imposter syndrome.   And he's a – I don't know,
    I think he's white.
He's definitely a man. Pretty privileged I'd say.
To make that very public declaration, you have to have
        that kind of comfort.

    And I think he definitely benefited from that because –
I'm not diminishing his feelings; I'm sure they were real
        and genuine – but what it made possible was for people
to rush in and say
    'No, don't feel like that. You're really capable.'

And then you get those reassurances.   Whereas if you don't
feel able to articulate it, or to be so public about it –
        putting it on Twitter's very public isn't it?
you're not going to get that reassurance.

Lolita

Well, my parents divorced when I was seven.
They had a really bad divorce.
My dad got remarried and my stepmum has three sons.
It's always been 'us' versus 'them'.
    And from when I was a kid I always had to show
that I was the strongest. Between me and my sister
I was the oldest.   I had to look after my sister,
            make sure there was no harm coming to her.

My parents used us children   as a way of having
arguments between them. My stepmum was a lot like that
as well. And a lot like: 'You can't do this because
you're a girl. You can't behave like this because
you're a girl.'   The boys are allowed to do everything.
    The boys can go out.   'You girls have to stay
home because you could get pregnant.' You know, all of
these things...

I'm OK to keep going.

I think it also impacts now on how I am as a mum.
When my babies were born the first thing I told
my dad was: 'I don't know how my mum could
    have left us, when she had this.'

And then I came to understand more about depression
and about mental health. These things.   I realised
that my mum had these problems, but she hadn't
had the support she'd needed.   Now me and my mum
are really close. Because I understand more about why
my mum did the things she did.   I realise that the things
my stepmum was saying and doing were not really...
right. But I've realised that in my family that's
the way we've been brought up.   You just toughen up.

Because otherwise
        you're going to be a burden on everyone.

Sinéad

When I was a child we moved around a lot, so I went

to lots of different schools. I was aware that I would often
do that kind of hanging on the edge of something,

holding back: at the back of the classroom, edge
of the game in the playground at break time.   I was often

involved in theatre, and, yeah, I would often feel like
everybody else was at home there and I was not.

I was sort of, peripheral… I don't really know
how to explain it.   I never committed fully to something.

I'd be there, but I would be…   protective. In case I was
found out… to be, you know, not really an actor.
        Not really… something.

Publisher

Dear Kate,

Since responding to *Pretenders* it's been worrying me
that something is missing in the construction of the
book – unless that's still be added – which I think may
prevent it from cohering. That missing element is Kate
Potts, you…

there's little sense of where the impetus for the book has come from, which must surely be your own experiences of – or anxieties over – imposter syndrome in one form or another. Not including yourself anywhere feels like an abstention or even a cop out which I think will puzzle or annoy reviewers and readers.

If you feel able to tackle this head on, one possible approach might be in a poem, or even a monologue of your own. If you were to respond to the questions you put to your interviewees, what would you say?

Kate

When did I first feel like an imposter?
I remember I didn't have a friend's phone number.
She'd gone to a different secondary school to me and I didn't have her number. She wasn't in the phone book.

My parents said 'Phone directory enquiries.' So I did that.
Does it still exist in the internet age?
I would have been about 11, I think. Dialling
    on the beige finger-dial phone we had sat in the hallway.

The woman said: 'Please stay on the line if you require
further assistance.'   I didn't realise that this meant
    if you wanted another number,   a different one.
I thought maybe they'd try something different to find the
    number you'd asked for at first.

I was really persistent. Or stubborn. I must have
really wanted to phone this friend!
I just asked for the same number again and again.
Eventually, I got a man very sternly telling me off who

thought I was just causing trouble.   A kid causing trouble.
I still remember the kick, the cringe of it.

Is that feeling like an imposter? It's feeling exposed.
Ashamed of your lack of knowledge and understanding.
      Like you've got something really, really wrong.

What else? I can remember… trying to go to the pub
very ineptly when I was about sixteen.   Pretending
I'd been before when I hadn't. I think I was trying
      to impress a boy.
      I *was* being an imposter. I was pretending to be part of a
grown-up world that I didn't understand.

Once, we went to the theatre, or tried to go to the theatre
      and my parents had accidentally – they were super-busy
with work – they'd got the wrong date.

      We walked into our local theatre, and we walked
down the long, red aisle to go to our seats
      and my dad said to the people sitting there,
'Excuse me, I think you're sitting in our seats.' It turned out
that actually,   we'd got the wrong day; our tickets
        were for a different day that had already passed.
So we'd missed the play.
                          We all turned round   and trooped
back up and out of the theatre and went home.

      Just that feeling of…   anticipation and thinking that you
belonged somewhere and that you had a right to be there,
        and then, recognising that actually, you didn't.
      Everyone knew you were making it up.
It was too good for you.

These things – getting told off by directory enquiries, having
no seats at the theatre – they're, I guess, not a cause but

30

what it feels like, for me.   To be an imposter.
Shame, I suppose. Which is probably what anyone
  would feel in those situations. But I felt –
recognised, permanently marked out, in those moments.

You're an imposter. You don't have a right to be there.

A Telephone Conversation with My Sister/ Footnotes

1.Your voice is muddy and loose. From the cadence of your 'what?' I can picture you: pint mug of tea, hand on hip at the window. The smudgy glass.

2. For *sister*, see mirror; see language comprised of silences.

3. I'm thinking of suitcases, rucksacks, freight: the process of bearing something from one place to another; *conveyance, transportation.*

4. 'Awake' is an effort, a doleful burden.
I don't mention the dream I've had in which you're dog-tired. You nod and nod, mechanical, leaden eyelids. I haul you onto my back like a woollen coat and set off for home.

5. We never set fire to the lawn with the magnifying glass. The scissor blades didn't draw blood. But aged five and seven, we loaded our possessions into plastic beach buckets and set out to seek our fortunes.

6. You didn't fall out of the bunk bed above me and break your leg, though it feels like a clear and genuine memory. The green-dyed hamster story is also invented. At school, we never acknowledged each other's presence.

7. In journal no.3, page 6, I narrate this journey home:

'On the morning bus back to London I prised my cheek
from the window-glass and spilled a coastline of dribble.

My eyes fell and fell back. Sleep was a rusty bullet –
my brain was a plumbing stone. I spoke, or dreamed I spoke,

aloud, but I couldn't catch any of the sense. The daytrippers
were creaseless, utterly peachy: *Look, it's Oxford Street!*

they said.

We were just past Earl's Court: a wide, nondescript avenue.'

8. And here's that silence again: the one with scuzzy, static
water dammed behind it, rising. I count the things said/un-
said. I riffle around for the right shaped question.

9. 'We conventionally represent translation as bridging two
languages, as a "communication model of equivalence and
exchange", but that is not what it is.' (Naoki Sakai qtd in
Mueke, Stephen, 'Preface', Cooke, Stuart (ed.) *George
Dyungayan's Bulu Line: A West Kimberley Song Cycle*
(Glebe: Puncher & Wattman Poetry,: 8).

10. This endless waiting at bus-stops occurs in subsequent stories and fragments. See journal 42, p8:

'The clock read 4.27am., and the house was quiet. A warm imprint on the sheets where the child's body had been.

Outside, on the landing, stock-still by the stair gate. She was waiting for the bus, she said. Had to get home.'

11. I was ashamed. How could I look the newspaper boy in the eye? My small, dull heart like a cherrystone. For guts, hardihood, flint and grit, see 'bitter kernel'.

12. I'm remembering taxiing home from that work party. Reams of night road, the recreation grounds of South London swooning by.

13. I've lost track of the sense of the words we are making. Our voices mimic the paper sound of reed-stalks jostling, mouthing a nameless sea-song.

14. Outside the babble of this conversation, a duo of synchronised geese rides the air. The geese twist gravity, tickle the lake. A mallard tips tail-up, powers its body under.

An iron tower spins out power lines across the afternoon, and the blue is porcelain tea-cup, afternoon kimono.

15. I haven't told you yet that while I was trying to read your email, my browser crashed repeatedly. The software company representative – his voice very protracted as if underwater – fiddled (remotely) inside my computer's intestines. When I restarted, as instructed, the screen blinked softly in a new mauve, looped a blank bloom of a reboot that wouldn't settle. I screamed, and then I spent two hours calling for my cat in the communal garden, rattling a paper bag of desiccated meat. Later I found her wedged, contented, inside the open suitcase underneath my bed.

16. I remember that party on the boat: Sherri measuring up the single men like someone compiling a battle plan; then us, snug, hip to hip, Lambada-ing through a dancefloor of investment bankers and their plastic surprise. Then later, my voice, as if ventriloquised from a smaller body, calling you from inside a grim, locked toilet cubicle: *I need you to find me; I don't know where I am.*

IMPOSTERS (1)

Grand Duchess Anastasia of Russia (Anna Anderson/ Franziska Schanzkowska)

1921. At Dalldorf Asylum, 'Madame Unknown' is mute, beset by visitors. They want to catch her out, or thrill with recognition.

She feigned death, hid among the bodies, escaped the basement at Ekatarinburg alive. Anastasia isn't bullet-riddled meat, a bonesack in blunt earth.

    (Also: the grenade never slipped and exploded, nobody died, Franziska's factory work went on with dull precision).

Many visitors want badly for her to be Anastasia, and many want badly for her not to be.

At Baron and Baroness von Kleist's, Zina Tolstoy picks out a waltz from Anastasia's childhood on the piano keys, and Anna crumples, heaving, sobbing.

'Do you play?' Zina asks. 'Do you recognise the music?'

Dr Otto Reche is certain: *Such coincidence between two human faces is not possible unless they are the same person or identical twins.*

'How shall I tell you who I am?' Anna asks 'In which way? Can you tell me that? Can you really prove to me who *you* are?'

Dwellings

I lived in a tall, thin house. There were guns in the basement, disco angels in the attic. We made murals of trees on the kitchen wall with our small handprints for leaves. At night I dreamed of foiled or thwarted escapes: a giant fist pulling me back. When I made it outside, my feet pistoned furiously on the pavement, but I stayed rooted to the spot.

When my niece makes a den (sofa cushions, chairs, a throw over the top) she wants us both inside it, fugitives breathing into the warmth – even though my limbs are enormous and I risk collapsing the structure. It's a womb and she wants us in it.

Once in a house, I watched myself from a high, cobwebbed corner. Two low beds pushed close. The plastic shower cupboard, slit of courtyard window. Our bodies were slung together like pink insects, skinny-legged, spawning. He was probably thinking of his future children, their glorious biceps – or nothing. I was a bruised cicada. Pinned bird bones.

I lived in a house with damp in its marrow. You could see your breath. Cracks lengthened and bled when the freight trains rocked past. The other woman who lived there was penitent. She wore black and ate cabbage soup. The front door swelled and stuck with sour clouds of her tears; I escaped through the kitchen window.

Along the canal path, the hillside swings into view. A man steps out onto the fire escape of a repurposed warehouse. We see each other and space opens up; the air is birdsong.

When televisions were dark, thick boxes, did I think of them as enchanted dioramas? Holding people, landscapes, shrunk inside them? Puppeteers' gloves manipulating under the cloth.

Once I lived with two men. We stole a cat to get rid of the mice. I loved my giant, wrought-iron bed but I couldn't keep up with the house and all its excretions and spillages. In the garden, roadkill rotted in buckets and rats swarmed over the vegetable scraps.

Once I lived six storeys up on the high road. I came off the pill and took bitter herbal potions to make my periods come. Bedbugs stuck to my wrists like bloody pearls.

And once, I lived in a kind house. There were pints of tea; there was karaoke at dawn. My bones thickened and I grew strong and tall, *like a tree firmly planted by streams of water. And my leaf did not wither.*

WORK,WORK, WORK

voices

Michelle

She says 'What is it you do again, Michelle?'
Well I'm called a lecturer, but you know, I'm just really
   a bit of a fake.

I dust my palms on my jeans.   I'm even uncomfortable
with the term, the names that you're called.   Maybe I'm not
a real one.   I feel slightly embarrassed to say that's my job.

What's a lecturer like? More authoritative than me.
A bit more serious. Maybe posher than me.
     Maybe without a Welsh accent.   That's really daft,
isn't it. It's interesting...

Oooh, I got a little smile!
   Are you waving, baby? Can he see me on the screen?

If something goes wrong at work it's a big drama.   It hurts
more.   Whereas, if I had more confidence, it might not be
as bad.   I don't know.   I'm speculating.
   It's that internal narrative:
Well, you shouldn't really be doing this job anyway. That's
what happens when you get out of your depth.

It's such a complex phenomenon really, isn't it. Just how
shifting it is. It's made me reflect.

I went to a staff development session on unconscious bias.

I thought 'Should I be here?' Because everyone else there
was quite senior. But then –

One minute I feel like an imposter – the next I think
   I know more than you do.

Lynn

I wrote something myself.   I can send you this if you want.
I mean, the writing looks like this... If you want me
to take a picture   or just kind of read it to you or something,
    then I'm quite happy to.

Often, I write something like this and think: 'Well,
I wonder if I wrote this.   Or if somebody else wrote it?'
You come across something and think,   'Yeah, that's very
good, that's really expressive.   But I wonder if I wrote it.
Or if I copied it out from somebody else's work.'
But actually, if I copy from somebody else's work I will
say it.   I will say, page 72 of such and such a book by such
and such a person. It's sometimes
        about not believing that things are mine.

In my work, I've not gone for things that have got my name
written on it. You know, as in   'This job is for you.
This situation is for you.' You know.   I've thought
'But is it really for you?' and then not applied myself.
I won't go for competitions or put myself forward,   swim
through it on my own. But if somebody asks me   to read,
I'll say yes.   Or would you submit for this, I'll say yes.

Jacob

I spoke to a saxophone player, a violinist, and the drummer
I toured China with, about your project.
    The feeling seems to be that musicians wouldn't want to
openly admit to imposter syndrome even if they felt it.
Maybe because

(although I guess we all feel it to some degree?) you can't
afford to even think it. You have to force it out of your mind.
    You have to focus and concentrate to perform.

Author

I find an app that can record phone calls and install it. In summer I do some interviews walking along the lush, green-hemmed canal path with my baby in a sling, or jiggling him under the enormous, wise old oak tree outside our new home.

When I go to play back the recordings, the interviewees' voices are a rustling, metallic whisper, so quiet I can hardly hear them. I can hear is the boom of my own questions and responses. It's as if I'm talking to myself.

Olivia

It's ridiculous because I'm aware that I'm doing fine.
I've got a good job, I'm doing, you know, all the right things.

Imposter syndrome impacts me in terms of –
I left nursing a couple of times, left to do
    something else.   But then went into something else
    and it followed me.
        I'm getting better over time, with age.

Do you want a biscuit?   I'll leave the packet here.

It sounds extreme,   saying this. But I'm being really open and honest.   At work I had some teaching, I was training some students, some junior colleagues –   I felt like,
    Who am I to be teaching these colleagues? Obviously
I had loads to teach them. It was fine when it was just them,
    but as soon as the practice manager was in earshot,
it threw me off. I really clammed up.   I got a dry mouth, sweaty palms.
        Quite an interesting response…

I thought   *God, I really need to get over this now.*

My dad died when I was 18 and then I went to uni.
I did the nursing degree   when I was 21. I'd just broken up
with my boyfriend of five years.   I had a lot going on.
        I took that into the degree with me.

It was a time   that was difficult. I was trying to do these
placements where they're assessing all the time and –
It felt personal.   When you go on a placement and they
assess you it's about you as a person:
        'Oh, be more confident, speak louder.'

And well, I'm a quiet person in my own way.

I had one particular placement – I had one placement,
my last placement.   It was the anniversary
    of my dad's death

and I was a little bit more stressed than normal. And I didn't
tell them.   It was a very badly set up placement. And then
    the next week, I got upset with a patient because –
this is the brief explanation –   they were difficult.
            And my educator there and then said,
'Right. You have to stop the placement now.'

So they cancelled the placement there and then, and I didn't
qualify that year. I had to do my placement in the summer
and then I qualified later.   It delayed everything.   And he'd
            made that decision in a minute.

So I think   I've always had that, *Oh well I qualified
six months after everyone else.*
        I didn't fail the placement but...

It's left a little,   a little nut in my brain that I'd somehow....
If the placement had been more supportive it would have

been OK.   So I think having the student who I've just had has brought that up a bit.   I've been trying to be really supportive of her –
          Probably over-supportive.
But I am getting better.
I'm saying all this,   I'm being really open and honest with you but, day to day, you wouldn't notice.
          That's the whole thing isn't it?

The dyslexia got assessed at uni. It might impact how I feel. If I'm a bit slow at processing things,   I can be a bit delayed and I think back and, I don't know the answer straight away but…   in a group situation
          I can be slower.

But that's not to say I'm not as good,
     it's just that I process things slightly differently. But that can make me feel like, *Oh, I –*

It came up at university. They're assessing you in a way that feels very personal. And they assessed me for dyslexia.
So I got that.

               And since then, other things I've noticed. So, yeah,
               processing slightly differently.

Is it really a fear of not fitting in,   and then a fear of being alone? A fear of being found out, not fitting in, not being good enough? So then the fundamental fear is that you're going to be   pushed away. It's the fear of
          being alone. It's rejection.

I didn't really think of the sociological bit. It's interesting. I'm blonde, I'm female. I did sport as a kid. I'm white and in the UK. That's me. So –

But going back to the learning differences.
There's a very set, procedural way to do things
in the NHS. And maybe that's what I don't fit in with.
        But I do, I'm doing it, so…

I'm finding it really hard to talk about.   I feel like I'm
saying   almost too much, but not quite getting to
the crux of it. It's quite hard to admit it, isn't it?
Because I'm telling you, basically, I think I'm a crap nurse.

But I don't think that. And that's quite a hard thing to say,
because I've been qualified for 10 years and –

I would never say it to anyone.
I don't want to be undermining myself.

Author

The edited transcript I email makes some of my
interviewees uncomfortable. They don't want to be
misrepresented, or uncomfortably exposed. 'Can you
take that out?' they ask. Or, 'Take that out,' they order.

I prefer to change key identifying details rather than
removing them completely. Otherwise, I'm left with
paper cut-out people and abstract voices. But I understand
the impulse to retract and to protect; I feel it too.

Peter

I'm terrible at job interviews. I'm not bad at getting
interviews but I'm terrible at them. It's that fear of
getting found out. It can make me less likely to put
myself forward for things.

There's a huge issue with me and self-promotion, which is
a massive problem when I've tried to get a sideline
as a freelance journalist. I've been doing freelancing
for *The Guardian*   and other things over the years.
Which is really great, but I'm terrible   at pushing myself
forward or promoting myself.

The same goes with my music; I'm very loath to promote
that at all. I think it's part of that idea that I'm not
going to live up to people's expectations,   I'm going
to oversell myself.

People are going to see through this, or think
I'm being really vain. Or arrogant.
In some respects, it's held me back.

And it's a different thing from lacking confidence.
It's more that other people might have
a different view from me about my abilities.

I'm really happy to promote other people.   I really love
supporting other people's creative ventures.

But when it comes to supporting my own stuff   I just think
it's paper thin. It's…. It's really fragile, it's brittle,
frail…

When I visited *The Guardian* offices there were these men
with nicely trimmed beards and slinky spectacles.
And I felt like Worzel Gummidge traipsing round.

And if I'm in a proper yokel pub in some remote location
        I will feel like Mr Guardianista there,
Mr Metropolitan.   Things flip about a lot.

Something about qualifications comes to mind. I have this
        quite keen sense… I think it's justified.
        Men like me have an easy time compared to a lot of
        people,   don't have to work nearly as hard
as a lot of people.

I have no sense of achievement. I was absolutely expected
        to go to university. My academic achievements have
        been pretty mediocre frankly.   But also, I'm left
        with a sense that my achievements are not fully
earned. It's made me quite keenly aware of a lack of –
        I don't know….

A thinness, or a hollowness, or a lack of substance, a sort of
        brittleness.   I sometimes feel like winter sun,
        the sun in January compared to the sun in July.
        There's a light there but the heat is missing.

I have to… I just have to pick up my cat and make sure she's
        not bothering my wife. She has a tendency to knock
        on my wife's door when she's
                on difficult phone calls.
        There we go! Sorry…

It may be doing myself down.   Actually *The Guardian*
        freelance work was earned. They had no idea who I
        was, what my background was. But I'm very aware
        of the advantages and privileges I've had.

I wonder what the opposite of imposter syndrome might be,
whether it's 'entitlement syndrome,' whether there's
something along those lines.

A lot of people who present as 'qualified' may feel this way.
I need to   expand my sense of awareness beyond myself.

Sinéad

   I never got over feeling like a newcomer. Even though
I worked in further education for, I don't know, twenty-
something years.   Or even more.

A very long time.   I taught English overseas early on,
in Japan mostly, and then I taught key skills communication.

I'm qualified. But I never quite got to the point where I felt,
or confidently felt,   I am an expert in this.

But sometimes, some people would say 'Wow, you know
a lot about this.' And I'd just kind of think, 'Yeah,

I suppose so.' Or I'd think, 'Yeah but it's not
rocket science.' I could never really get to a point where I

could welcome that feedback. Although I have tried.
                I made a move into higher education

as a dyslexia specialist.   I feel apologetic –
but 'dyslexia specialist' is what people with my qualification

are called. I feel I have to explain: *Don't get me wrong,*
I'm not saying I'm a specialist...

And, in the institution that I work in now, people
introduce me and say, 'Sinéad's our dyslexia specialist,'

and I think 'Don't ask me any questions!' Maybe that's
a lack of confidence as well… Even though I know

if somebody asked me a question, I could
answer it. I couldn't do it perfectly, but I could do it. I think

that's the way I was brought up, brought up not to be
boastful, to be self-deprecating.   And I think

because of words like 'academia', it always feels
like somebody has the secret to it all, and it's not me.

   In higher education I've done freelance work. I've been
based in two institutions – one very big university in Leeds

– and never got the hang of the institution. I always was
curious about the people who did:

how did they know all that they knew? I never really
understood.   There's been a sense

of never quite being part of the real institution,
the inner circle of something. In the past I've let it get

the better of me – you know, I've shied away from things,
taken a back seat.   But now I try to think, you know,

it doesn't matter. It doesn't really matter if I am an
imposter. Some people become – prime minister –

and they *should* feel like imposters. But I kind of think, well,
what does it matter?   I still have something to contribute.

I don't think I wanted to work in theatre, even though
that was my degree. I definitely felt like an imposter

in theatre, because you need to be a certain person.
It's kind of outgoing. Quite pushy. A lesson plan is a bit like

a script. You're deciding what you're saying, how will
the audience respond.   It's a performance.

I come from quite a big family and there was a lot
of teasing and kind of, not being allowed   to take yourself

very seriously. Which obviously has got good things about it.
   But recently….   Now that I'm talking about it

I think a lot of this is just so bound up
with confidence.   But I have been doing an online zoom

open mic thing. And that's based in the US. And, you know,
all the time, I feel like an imposter there. Partly

because so many of them are American. But some are
   English, some are Scottish…

They're all incredibly welcoming. But I just have this sort of
thing that, yeah, they'll discover I'm not really   a poet.

And that has been quite a big thing for me to work
towards saying *I'm a poet.*   There was a meet-up

with some of these people in London and we went,
and it was lovely, but you know again, just… I… feel like

there's something much more genuine about everybody else.
I haven't done an MA in creative writing or poetry.

I feel like that's the secret, now, that I've planted
in my head. I'll never be good enough unless I do an MA

in creative writing, which I can't do because I can't afford it.
I can rationalise it,   but if I'm not careful

it's a feeling that will overwhelm me... When I've done in-
person classes I've quite often not said anything

because   I feel like I'll say something stupid. And then
kind of just enjoy the things other people have said, stupid

or otherwise. You know, it's all interesting. It's all part of
a discussion. So I know that it's not rational

or sensible. I mean it might be sensible,   in terms
    of protection.

                I feel like lots of things that I am: a woman,
a mother, a poet. A teacher, even. They're all sort of quite

vulnerable to ridicule somehow.   Or kind of, jokiness.
And I'm a bit…. I guess I'm wary of that.   It's making

me think I want to read more about what
imposter syndrome really is. Where it comes from. I think

one of the things is, in my current job, I've been there in the
covid lockdown. So physically, it hasn't been possible

to feel really part of something.   Everybody's
on different hours.   There are very few people there.

There's a canteen that nobody, well, certainly staff, rarely
sit in. And you don't meet people

in the corridors. And then at the other university
I was in, everyone was massively stressed and, yeah, quite

pissed off. So even if you did pass someone
in the corridor it wasn't 'Oh, hello,' it was   'Oh

I'm so stressed. This is so awful. The university
are behaving so badly.' So yeah.

Author

In Kazuo Ishiguro's novel *Never Let me Go* the action
takes place in an alternative England where human
clones are used to prolong the lives of non-clones
through their 'harvested' vital organs. Part of the book's
horror comes from the flat resignation of its clone
narrator, Kathy, who has been raised within this
system and its institutions. I find it impossible to
remember this book without thinking of the UK's
histories of colonialism and class, although the
narrative leaves itself open for other resonances.

At Hailsham, the boarding school where Kathy grows
up, the pupils are encouraged to make art. Kathy's
friend Tommy comes to believe that this artwork,
might prove them to be creatures with unique souls
rather than thin copies – and so worthy of being
released from their grim duties as 'donors'.

I suppose all art can serve this function: self-expression,
a means of trying to outsmart mortality. But I recognised
too, when I first read the novel, the need to make art as
a stay against violence, a way of trying to prove myself
fully human.

Tiffany

        I'm remembering turning up for that course
at the Soho theatre –

a sudden blast from the past. That's an early one.

     Even though I should have been proud of myself
        for having made the shortlist, getting
onto the course, I was looking at people around me,
        thinking 'Everyone looks so
    intelligent and creative'. Perceiving that from
        how people looked –   that's just crazy.
I mean, I was still at university, doing my BA.
  I was 21. Before that
    I was applying for drama school. I didn't really know
    what, or who, I wanted to be.
You're on speakerphone, but there's no one else here.
    I don't know if you can hear me properly?
I'm a bit throaty. I'm just getting over a virus.

I was studying theatre,   aiming to become
  a playwright. I felt very much equal to my peers. I was
ambitious. There was no voice in my head telling me I didn't
    belong. When I –

    I had a breakdown because I couldn't write, a few
jobs, and so forth.
    I reassessed my life and I thought *I'm going to write
    poetry again but this time take it seriously*, because
I couldn't write the plays I wanted to.

    So I think, actually,
    the first time I felt like an imposter was during that Soho
Theatre course. The first time someone put trust in me,
handed me

an opportunity. You spend your whole life trying
to achieve something, and then   when someone gives
    you an opportunity or praise – you ingest that negatively.
You think, 'Oh actually, do I deserve that?'

It's something you carry with you quietly. Day to day.

I had potential.   It's natural to question your place
and self-worth when you're thrust into a new –
    structure, put to the challenge.
        But my poetry was published straight away
            and I took that as a sign.
    I'm going to be a poet. This is my destiny.

I'd written poetry in my youth and at school
    and enjoyed it. So this happened. I didn't feel unequal
    at all. I felt ambitious and explorative and quite naïve
and probably childlike at the time. A little bit romantic.
Everything was great!

    I met a few people on the poetry scene. I got more
        deeply involved. I went to study poetry as an MA
            at Kingston. But around this time, I started to question
                my self-worth as a writer.   From an intellectual
        standpoint as much as any other. I realised I'd been
            a little bit naïve with my work.   I wasn't
                as good as many of my peers on the writing scene.
            I needed to prove myself.   I can't pinpoint it,
    but this is when I started to feel   like I didn't really belong.

        I had to keep proving myself to myself, not just
my peers. I was… I had the sense
that people looked down on me – as if I was this silly girl –
who just
    wanted to play at being a poet rather than being a poet.

I think it's very much to do with belonging. We're all trying
     to belong, in a sense, aren't we?

It's not owning yourself, not owning your own voice,
     not owning your own work.
          Not believing you deserve positive feedback
     or praise.

And this has continued,
     to a lesser extent, throughout my career. Because of
my disorder, I experienced a very belated coming of age.
     Now I realise more of my self-worth.
          I've grown up, I suppose.
          It's been   over a decade. I wish
things had been different... I was battling depression
     at the time.

It was very hard for me to see past that.

I feel the need to show people I'm still of value.
I see people doing it, people I love, writers, artists, actors.
There's   a fear of disappearing, not being seen.

Author

I don't want to over-interpret the voices; I want them
to speak for themselves. I'm sceptical of the idea of
authors 'giving voice' in their books – as if voice is
something that can be philanthropically gifted. I want
the voices in the collection to ring clear on their own
terms, not to be coopted, used or exploited by me.

But, of course, they can't stand alone. I'm already part
of the picture. Or, more accurately, standing behind the
lens and framing all the shots. I'm there in my own
un-recorded responses, in the text patterns; my breath
on every page.

Kate

I did a terrible, terrible interview for a job that was
my dream job, a long time ago.

It was a university lecturing job.   I'd only just started
my PhD so really, I was underqualified.   But I felt like
an absolute fraud. I couldn't believe I was there,
    and I think it really came across in the way
I did the interview.   I was working at the same university,
but in the office. I didn't have any interview clothes,
    so I'd borrowed a dress from my sister which, once I got
there,   just felt wrong.   It was polka dot with frills,
from H&M. Quite thin.   And I felt like I just
didn't know what I was doing. I felt really exposed, naked.
And really ashamed. That they would all see
that I didn't know what I was doing.

And I think it's….   there's stuff to do with background,
and there's stuff to do with….
I didn't go to a particularly great secondary school,
although I went to university after that.
There's this feeling of not knowing, not having had the right
education, on some level… not having
the knowledge and skills required to know what's expected,
and to navigate social situations, especially.

I mean, job interviews are terrifying anyway, but I felt…
    I think I can become   almost angry, in those situations.
I was so desperately trying to prove that I was someone
    who could be considered for the job because I felt   so
incapable, and so teenage,   in that moment.

In my twenties I did teacher training –
FE college teaching. English. It was really brilliant,

and scary. Then fifty- or sixty-hour weeks
on a zero hours contract. Just keeping going on adrenaline.
Constant performance. The kids
were energetic, pushing the boundaries.
    Sometimes threatening.   When I got more confident,
something odd happened. In the middle of a class
    when everything was going well – a group really enjoying
a discussion, or an activity – I'd get this sudden, glassy
    feeling of absolute doom. Cold sweat. I felt as if I couldn't
speak. Or breathe.   I kept going, somehow.

My GP referred me for 10 weeks of NHS therapy.
I remember the therapist turned up
    in black motorbike leathers, usually.
We talked about guilt, and self-sabotage. Didn't I
        deserve better?

'It's not about what you deserve,' my mum said.
        Which irritated me, at the time.
    In lots of ways, though, she's right.

I think it's definitely affected me... it's definitely
affected my job applications.   The idea that I've just,
kind of, blagged my way in somehow.   I think, in the past,
there's been this feeling of not deserving...
kindness. And in terms of career?   I mean, there are
issues to do with trying to do   something quite competitive,
just the practical logistics of that. Years of study, not earning
much. But then,   having more confidence
    in my own abilities and self-worth –
there are times when that really would have helped.

In the past, if I wrote something and I knew it was working
quite well, it was almost as if I hadn't written it.   As if
it had come through me from somewhere else.
It wasn't actually me.

It's tricky. Where does imposter syndrome end
and where does anxiety begin?

Sometimes in parent and baby groups   I've felt a bit like...
I went out for lunch around Christmas time last year
with a bunch of women I'd met
at a kids' music and storytelling group.
When everybody else starts talking about their families
and their partners...   It's just   a different experience.

There are plenty of single parents in the world. But, yeah,
just this idea   that I'd kind of blagged my way in there,
        somewhere I wasn't quite supposed to be.

Tabitha

Don't get me wrong – I definitely think imposter syndrome's
a bad thing, on balance. But there are these weird angles
where actually   it forces you to think critically,
        to move out of your comfort zone.

I think it made me feign a bit of confidence.

You just keep trying to do more things and trying to impress
people.   Which is exhausting and not the way it should be.
But in the process you do...   learn new skills.   Hopefully
you gain some perspective   on what it is you can do,
how capable you actually are.

It was three and a half, four years ago   When I started
my job at my healthcare trust – in pharmacy.
    And I was there on promotion... Yeah, I definitely
felt, definitely felt   imposter syndrome quite strongly.
But I didn't really... appreciate it was imposter syndrome.
    Or maybe I did, maybe I was aware of it.

Is the reception bad there? OK, great. I can hear you.

I thought I just wasn't capable of doing the job
    I was there to do – I felt like I was acting up.
Whereas with the benefit of hindsight I can see that
    I was more than capable.

It was a little bit of an unusual situation.   There should
have been a few more layers of management above me
but there weren't. There was a bit of a…   a vacuum.
    So actually I was having to do things and go to things
that typically   I wouldn't have had to have done.

Meetings with CEOs, quite high-powered people. It was a bit
of a perfect storm… But looking back at those meetings,
I think actually what I had to say was just as valid.   I just
didn't have the self-belief at the time. Looking back,
    I want

to pinch myself   for some of those times
    when I should have just said it, gone for it.

Imposter syndrome propels and forces you…
You're in a situation where you're trying to prove yourself
    to people, you're kind of…

I'm not articulating it very well.   Here's an example.
There was a time I was doing some research work. I was
leading a team of four and there were 100-odd
    colleagues to support.

    There was too much. We were under-resourced.
Over-capacity, under-resourced.   And somebody wanted
some very specific data analysis done on antimalaria drugs.
    I didn't have the expertise to do it, or the time.
So I said no, quite forcefully –   more forcefully
    than I would do now.

I was quite honest, I just said: 'Look, we don't have
the skills to do this, or the time.'

I learned that I could go to those meetings with high-
powered people and looking back, actually it was fine.

I had an interview for a job recently and I didn't get it.
    I had some really helpful feedback.   It was a
promotion and a very specialist pharmacy role.

They said that my technical knowledge was actually OK,
it was borderline. What let me down was actually
my communication and leadership stuff,   and I thought
        Oh, that's strange! Because actually

    I feel way more confident about that than the technical
stuff.   So that's an example for me of where the imposter
feelings seeped into my general performance,
        worked against me.

I've started doing a course for women –
    it's called *Closing the Gap* –   acknowledging the fact
that we are more likely to feel things like imposter
syndrome,   not have the same advantages as men,
feel less confident...

I think if you look at a workplace this plays out in women
being less senior, feeds into the gender pay gap and so on.

    When we went round and did our intros –   I can't
remember how big the group was... over ten.
Every single person referred to their imposter syndrome
    in some way.

I didn't feel imposter syndrome in that instance
because everybody had it. Which felt quite freeing and
liberating.

I thought *Ah, this is great. I'm tackling it head on.*

But then after that with the interview I thought *No –*
 I'm still, still spiralling.

And in the lead-up to an interview – I don't know if you get
this? – I'll have a few days of panicking once I'm preparing.
And then eventually I'll get calmer and be able to
        make progress.

But what happened with this particular interview was
that I never really got out of that panic.   I got stuck
in a downward spiral.   I'm really rambling....
        I'm not really sure I've   answered your question?

        Where do the imposter feelings come from?
I think there are definitely societal factors. It's reinforced by
what you see. If you don't see people like you in positions
    of power –

or you see them to a lesser extent –   I think that's
definitely a factor. I think there's also the internal drive:
personality, psychological factors.
        I think it's also political.   It's a combination of who
you are as a person and external, societal, cultural influences.

I went to, you know, a state school.   It's always quite
striking when you meet people who went to...   not all
private schools,   but some privately educated people,
        they just have a certain.... They seem very self-assured.
Regardless of whether that's really reflective of what's going
on inside, there's a projection
        of confidence.

I think probably race is a factor – or definitely is.
Maybe not so much for me but for I think for people who...
for other people

of colour, I think. For someone I mentor,   I know it's
a real –   a real driver for her.   If you're a person
of colour and you're in a space that's pretty white, you just
feel like   you're not meant to be there. You don't see
yourself represented.
          You're an imposter.

In my workplace it feels like the higher up you get more
privileged people are. The frequency of people
          called *Tarquin* increases....
People who don't identify with that quite narrow
demographic   are more likely to have imposter feelings.

When I feel like an imposter, I think I've got
the power to take a step back, reflect on why... and then try
not to feel that way.

I think that's a personality thing.   But it's also somewhere
close to privilege. So maybe it's socially constructed too.

Author

As I begin to collect the interviews, I realise I'm
avoiding writing about my own imposter feelings –
while (supposedly) writing a book about imposter
feelings. Hiding at the back, scuffing the floor with my
black school lace-ups.

The only way to deal with my discomfort around
these interviewer/ interviewee power dynamics is to
make them visible, which means making myself
visible. Being the Author.

Lolita

I feel like I should be able to do everything myself.
And if I can't do it by myself   then there's.... something
wrong with me. It's not the workload that I have
or the fact that I juggle so many different things –
     it's that there's something wrong with me.

I mean, I feel like an imposter half...three quarters of the time
     to be honest! You know?

The most recent time   was when I was editing
my book.   Sometimes I get those highs and lows
when I'm reading a part of what I've done
     and I think 'What are you doing?'   And then I'm
thinking 'Is it even worth it? Should I even bother?'
I've got a box in my cupboard where   I've got all
of my edits – well, not all of them –
          they are printed out in that box. I riffle through that.
I realise how far I've come already. That gives me
the boost that I need –
     without having to talk to lots of other people.

It's very silly when you think about it because it's
just a bunch of papers. But it's so valuable because
I can see the setbacks, the wins and losses. The learning in
process. It's going to get there –
     it just needs time.

And especially now in art: you see all of this great
content on Instagram and Facebook,   on social
media. You see the finished picture and you think
     *Oh my god this is so good,   I'm never going
to be able to do that.*   We don't see the amount
of hours the person actually put in,
and the research, the ups and downs   of the artist
while they were making that one piece.

We just see the finished product and we think, either
        That's really easy for them to do, or *That's very*
hard for us to do.   I was saying the same thing to my
husband about books. Because now I can see first-hand
    how much work goes into writing just one book.

When I say I'm studying Creative Writing in uni,
a lot of people say: 'What's the point?
You're just writing.   Surely you can do that
by yourself, you're wasting your money.'

That's why I appreciate it so much when I'm doing
my edits at the end of the academic year. The writing
that I was doing at this time last year   has changed
so much. There is a difference   I can see the
difference.   So it's not just a one-person job.

Eve

The first time I felt like an imposter?
I remember, really vividly actually, being asked
    to do some lectures.
I'd wanted an academic career and I had… I think
I'd finished my PhD. I was near to finishing. Anyway,
I was asked to do some lectures on critical theory.
I'd never really had nerves before about things like that,
and I remember feeling really overwhelmed with nerves.
And feeling like an imposter. So, of course, I massively
overprepared,   in the way that you do.
    And all of the lectures that I did ended up being voted
'lecture of the year' by the students…

    But I just remember this really intense feeling of
What the hell am I doing here?

Oh my God, I always feel like an imposter as an artist.
Sometimes in my day job but less so now.

I've deliberately kind of massaged my job –
I've worked freelance since 2005 – I've deliberately
created a working environment which means
that I don't have to be too high status or take on
too many responsibilities, because I want to do my art
    on the side.   So the photography is where
my imposter syndrome tends to come in.

        It's when I'm reaching for something.

I got to the point where I had such strong feelings of
imposter syndrome that it was making me feel
    a bit crappy about my images. I chose
not to go to the studio. For kind of self-care reasons.
I decided to take a break. Sometimes, I'll just withdraw.

A lot of the time, all anybody really needs is somebody close
to say 'You're doing a good job,' or 'You're enough.'
        You know?

I had a really lovely chat the other day with
    a fellow photographer who's been around the block
many more times than I have. He was saying
        he's got to the point with his work
where he's just happy   to treat each new piece
like a flower in a garden.   It blooms for its season.
If you're lucky someone will come along and admire it.
    And then it fades. And that's enough.

Coping with Redundancy

In the *Visualising Your Future* session, I imagine a tightrope walker at the circus. The soles of my feet are chalky leather. I whisper sweetnesses to cajole the rope. Below is a sea of wide eyes and open mouths. There's no safety net. Every step is a bargain with calamity.

'That sounds very pressured,' says Michaela.

This morning I mistakenly walked into the room opposite this one and asked, 'Is this the coping with redundancy session?' Seven or eight white, middle-aged men were drinking coffee, their limbs and papers splayed over an enormous oak table scattered with empty cups, half-eaten pastries, gnawed fruit. The walls were panelled with what looked like maple.

'Make time for hobbies,' says Michaela. 'Some people find meditation helpful. Enjoy small wins; embrace the bigger picture.'

Co-trainer Martin's approach is more direct: 'Remove negative emotions from your cerebral cortex. If they surface, like ferrets, whack them down with a mallet.'

It began when I noticed my work allocation dwindling like grey bathwater draining away. Or my work being given to shinier colleagues. When I tried to contribute in meetings my voice came out of my line manager's mouth as if he was possessed.

I asked my line manager 'What should I do?' He said: 'Just keep tidying the database.' He is using the staff hours freed by my departure to make himself full-time *Head of Head of I'm In Charge Here*.

Redundancy's just an acceleration, Martin says, of our inevitable progress towards decay, our entropy. And aren't we all, in the end, rotting or carbonised meat? You might notice your cells depleting. You might feel your energy leach like a slow drip, like a leaky faucet.

'Thanks so much for all your hard work and dedication; we really appreciate your work, the way that you did...
          ...the work that you did,' the HR manager will say in the final (Zoom) meeting.

And then: her giant face filling the screen, frozen, lunging for 'end meeting'.

IMPOSTERS (2)

James Gray (Hannah Snell)

'There are no Bounds to be set to Love, Jealousy or Hatred.'

> *The female Soldier. Or, the Surprising Life and Adventures of Hannah Snell, born in the city of Worcester...*
> Anonymous (1750)

What did I expect? Not a townhouse and 6 children. He was bristly, tottering in thick, pink skin. At night, his fingers could make me bay like a stray dog, or weep.

One James Summs, a sailor, a Dutchman, turn'd out the worst and most unnatural of Husbands...

He called me 'angel' and 'treasure'. He told me sagas of the high seas. I was sallow and knackered. I knew of his roving; I had him anyway.

...who not only kept criminal Company with other Women of the basest Characters, but also made away with her Things, in Order to support his Luxury, and the daily Expences of his Whore.

He made an elopement from her.

I wouldn't be left to wait like a faithful dog.

Giving a full Scope to the genuine Bent of her Heart, she put on a Suit of her Brother-in-Law, Mr. James Gray's, Cloaths...

Those Things I put on! Like armour. I felt strength grow in my muscle. I imagined an inch, a rudder, at my crotch. 'James Gray,' I said to the mirror.

On the road, I became harder meat, more apparent. Tipped
hats and 'Good morning', none of the usual weazeling.

...and set out on the 23d of *November*, 1745, and
travelled to Coventry, with a View of finding her Husband...

I wouldn't be left to wait.

...where she enlisted on the 27th of the said Month
of November, in General Guise's Regiment, and in the
Company belonging to Captain Miller.

The suit was a sorcery. 'Sir,' they said. 'Come on now, lad.'

My hand signed the papers. 'Mr James Gray'. A map, an
ocean, opening, ample and vast like an August sky
  for Mr James Gray.

IMPOSTERS (3)

Anna Delvey (Anna Sorokin)

'I guess there are a lot of people who are not in their right mind in New York.'

Anna Sorokin, interview for *60 Minutes Australia*

It started with a crisp $100 dollar bill.

If someone is impressed by a $100 bill, I don't know what to tell them.

She was at all the best parties. A sweet girl, very polite.

I don't see myself as, exactly, a ladder-climber. The people at the top, they did not strike me as too talented, so I just thought, well, why....?

A sort of *Sound of Music* Fräulein wearing really fancy clothing: Balenciaga, or maybe Alaïa. Celine, Alexander Wang.

I don't care what you think of me. I don't need your approval; I don't need to impress you.

'Stop sinking into your body,' the trainer commanded. 'Shoulders back, navel to spine. You are a bright woman; you want to be a businesswoman.'

I'm trying to change the narrative. I feel like I deserve a second chance.

She announced she'd agreed a lease on 281 Park Avenue South, had plans for an arts centre, an exhibition space.

So many businesses are a house of cards. You just don't know about it.

People were like, *Okay, whatever.* She only ever paid with cash. 'In addition to $25m existing...' she wrote.

I never wanted to be famous.

'I feel like you are in a little over your head,' the trainer offered.

If I were to be prosecuted for similar crimes in Germany, I don't think people would really care.

Germany is worse than jail.

'Everyone was there. Like, Bill Gates was there.'
For a little while, she watched through the glass,
　　　　　then slipped in and mingled among them.

Shipwreck / The Iron Lady

Now you're   airless   suspended –
iron-armoured   under
the big blue/   swampy monolith,
 a sodden cache of newsreel
   in which   you shimmer and flare:
podium-ready, steely-eyed, jaw
jutted;   floral dress
in a flashbulb shower.

That voice: the one they called
   'cat sliding down a blackboard'
becomes   mellifluous, low,
       an LP of your
former self,   spinning, slow
   on the turntable.   You resist
   the blandishments of faint hearts.

We don't want to admit there's
a body here,   your picked-clean
fingertips, kn[c]ccaps, slack   belly,
bird-bone clavicle.
   Still, you exhort *initiative,*
   energy, the will to improve and
innovate as well as to preserve.

Even in death   you squeeze your
sleep in to four, thick hours.
   You still   the sore bird-
heart that quivers   your ribs. You're
resolute   after bombings, air-strikes,
    the hotel's near collapse.

Life   *is a reciprocal business.*
The point   was to change
    the world, not understand it.
                   There
are individual men and women and
there are families.   There are people
     who look to themselves first.

And you're   worm-thread and fossil,
sediment,   *no*   *soft*
option   no *hankering.*

BODIES / CARE

voices

Lynn

I felt like an imposter when I had my baby in the hospital.
She had a beautifully round caesarean-born head,   huge blue
eyes. I questioned   if she was mine. And if   at some point
   they'd take her away from me.

           There was a cruel nurse in the hospital who said
in the middle of the night,   'You'll never feed that baby!'
She was born early – an arranged caesarean.
                                          She was breach.
The trouble with feeding didn't resolve   until three weeks
later, with the help of a breastfeeding counsellor, some NCT
equipment. The nurse's hateful remarks   did nothing
for my confidence. At home we had,   what are those
things called? A sterilising unit.   I'd just come
out of hospital. And I had this idea that –

I think I was a bit psychotic but maybe only   for about
two days – (god, that's a memory) –
Even though I knew I was this child's mother,   I thought
I would be deemed not good enough.   I had this ridiculous
idea that my partner's mum   or someone else
would take her away from me.

From the minute, in pregnancy, that somebody   touches
your tummy, says 'Ooh can I feel this,'   and they've
already felt it, you feel – not your own property.
           Not good enough.

Of course, that's not the beginning.
I've tried to go back to where   the beginning possibly
could be. And the threads are more   and more tenuous.
Memory becomes more and more tenuous.

Olivia

Last week I saw a patient who I wasn't sure about.
    Osteoarthritis. Quite complex, and in a lot of pain this time.

    So I managed to get her booked in to do a new assessment
with a doctor. But I worried about it the day before:
'Oh gosh he's going to see that I've been doing completely
the wrong thing.' I missed something. He's going to say,
why have I booked her in,
            wasting his time?

Of course I hadn't. He assessed her, 'You're doing the right
thing. Carry on. Everything you're doing is fine. It was good
that you checked in.'   And I felt so much better after that.
            But I'd had that feeling of: he's going to find me out.

He's going to think *Why is this woman even qualified?*
            And that's ridiculous isn't it. It's tiring!

A bit of self-doubt is healthy, but there's got to be a balance.
I'm trying to think how imposter syndrome has been helpful.
    I'm sure it must have been   in some way.

Peter

I feel like an imposter quite a lot in church.

Certain things are assumed about your beliefs. Men's things.
        I went to an awful men's Christian group.
        Which is even worse than it sounds. I felt
        that not only was I an imposter as a Christian,
    but I was an imposter as a man.

I'm lucky enough to have a sense of the variability
          of masculinity I think, but all the imagery was of
          ropes and mountains and corrugated iron. I'm quite
          comfortable with my own brand of masculinity but I
felt like, *I don't even qualify as a man*   *in these circles.*

It's very hard to think of situations where I haven't felt
          on the outside of things.

It's an interesting philosophical question.
You could argue that it suggests a lack of empathy. It's about
          appreciating the subjectivity of others, like:

> *Oh, I'm sure these people might be just as scared as
> I am really, might be, may well be feeling what I'm
> feeling…*

Lolita

          You get that voice
that goes: 'Mmmm. Nah, you're not qualified for this.
          You don't speak English well enough.'

I think, professionally speaking
I have that *Fuck it* attitude.   I'm not going
to listen to this. I can do it.   And if I can't do it
then –   whatever. So it's more of a do it until
you can do it thing.   Fake it till you make it…
Professionally, as a librarian,
    I can always go to my manager if I need advice.
As a parent I think it's a lot more difficult.

I can go to my parents,   and my parents are not
unbiased. They'll be like,   'Oh yeah you're
doing fine.'   So for me that negates the proof
that I can do it.   They're just saying that

out of love, not because I can do it. But then
when people who know my children say
    'Oh my god these children are so well-behaved. They are
doing so well and they're lovely to be around,'
    I think, 'Well I can't be doing that badly.'

            It's a very needy thing, I think. Needing someone
to tell you: 'Oh yeah you're doing well.' It's really odd

Because I don't think of myself as needy. Thinking of it
that way, it's a very sour feeling.   I don't really
like it.   Because I see myself as someone
who's strong,   who's got the shoulders to deal
with being a mum, being a sister, being a daughter,
being – all of what makes me.   I don't really tend
to ask for help.   I'd feel guilty asking.
And I think,   somehow,   that relates
    to the imposter syndrome as well.

Even when my husband tells me, 'Look, you're
struggling with something;   let's ask for help,'

            from my family for example, with looking
after the kids, I'll say, 'No, I don't need the help.'
My husband is very supportive of everything that I do.
But I feel like I can't ask, I shouldn't ask.

I think society pushes that onto us: the way that we're
brought up, the way school works… all of that feeds
into this feeling, this
            'OK, I need to do it by myself.'

My husband's from India. He can ask his family
for things. For me, it's like, 'I can't ask my parents
for money. It's just not happening.'
I think that's where you see

the difference of cultures and different approaches.
I'm sure it has an impact.

It gets to the point where I struggle to ask for help
even if I know I need it.
The fact that I'm here by myself – my whole family is back
in France – it feeds into that idea of *I'm independent.*

I mean, I'm not counting my husband because obviously
that's different.　　　　But in terms of family, I can't say,
　　　　　'Let's pop in to Grandad's for a bit.' You know,
All that kind of thing. I can't
do that. And then asking for help from friends – it feels
like I shouldn't, because they've got their own lives
and they're busy, and, er… clearly, I should be able
　　to do it all by myself.

I don't know how many times my friends have told me:
'We're here. If you need help just give us a call.'
But it's really hard to take that step.

I know that my sister sees a –
　　　　　a shrink now. She was telling me that
it would be beneficial for me to. And some days I think
Yeah, maybe I should. But the other days I'm just like,
　　Mmmm, no – I don't need it.

But that feeling of *I'm fine* kind of backfires half the time.
It's during those days where everything feels bad. I've had
a fight with the kids – something like that.
　　　I feel like I'm rubbish at everything. *What's the point.*
All of these things.

I don't think it's just imposter syndrome. It's just –
I want it to be tomorrow. I think it's a lot of things

tied up together.   I started bullet journalling
recently and it actually helps.   I get to be creative
in a way that I'm not showing to everyone.
I can mess up, and it's fine.   Even if I have a bad day,
I can put   those thoughts into the journal.
It's not going to judge.

I like spending time with my kids, goofing around.
I think kids are very empathic. My two are.
They can feel when I'm not having a good day.
They'll come and say   'Mummy, do you want me
to do your hair?'   And I'll think, *Let's do that.*
Let's watch a movie, or play cards,
or do drawing or painting, or something. Doing that
together – it lifts me up.   I don't need
anyone else to be telling me whether what I'm doing is right
or wrong. I'm happy with what I've got.

The kids really help me. And walking in the forest.
Grounding myself back into what's important.

But if I stay by myself in the house   where there is
no music, no nothing –   I think that's where the imposter
syndrome is strongest.   It really shouts.
    You're rubbish at everything.   It gets hard.

When I'm feeling like this I go and ask my husband
for a hug.   Such a silly little thing, but it's the best
feeling. Otherwise, I call my mum, talk about why
I'm so down.   We figure it out.

I'm hoping that –   the way we're bringing up kids
now – they're not going to have imposter syndrome.
My son, I don't tell him – I heard my uncle one day
saying to my cousin,   'A boy doesn't cry.'
One time my husband said,   'Oh stop crying
like a girl.'   For him it was just a normal comment.

I said 'Don't say that. Don't even think
of saying that again.' I looked at my son and said,
        'If you want to cry, you cry. There's no problem
with crying.'

    All this talk of 'Oh, you've got to toughen up;
you've got to be stronger because of everything life is going
to throw at you. And because the world is not safe
    for a woman…'
    That makes me really angry, because I think that's exactly
how I became like this. People not trusting in themselves,
feeling like asking for help is for the weak… I'm hoping
    that changes.

Author

These interview texts are not, I realise, testimonies in
the legal sense of the word but something more fluid,
social, and interconnected. The narratives we tell
ourselves about our lives are provisional and evolving.
The self is a slippery fish.

Nevertheless, these conversations are true records of
particular times and places, perceptions, and memories.
The stories we tell ourselves about our lives are power-
ful, in part, because we can rewrite them.

Sinéad

Being a working mother is quite an uncomfortable thing.
People say,   'Oh it's great that you do that.'

But you just think: *would you think it was great*

to watch me sliding through mud?   It was kind of rough.

You know, it's not… It wasn't a great experience
or anything. I don't have any… Well no,

I do have regrets about the way I handled it all.
But my kids are grown up now.   You know, I'm glad

that I was able to keep going. Education was brilliant
for that, especially further education.

I had holidays off with my children. I had
nice managers who would let me go home to pick them up.

And things like that. So I had…   So I was very lucky
in that sense. But I never felt good about it.

I felt bad that I was somehow, kind of
costing them something.   I've often worked part-time,

and often felt like I'm just catching up, in between work
and parenting and not doing either all that well.

I guess that probably is a shared experience.

Kate

My parents are from backgrounds where there was,
or there has been – and this is partly a generational thing –
there's been in the past some quite, well, what I would
think of as poverty. Especially my mum.

    And this is partly about postwar rationing and all of
that, so I imagine it's pretty common across that generation.
But there's a sense of shame.

I didn't realise until recently that my parents overstretched
to buy their first house,   spent their last pennies,   and then
mortgage rates went up and they were really, really
struggling for a while.   I have these memories of kind of…
The settee was brown corduroy and wood. We didn't have
radiators in all the rooms in our house at first. And…   Just a
kind of   tension and stress
    around money.   But my dad, well my dad
was a university lecturer   and my mum was a teacher so….

But yeah, there's this competing stuff around… they had
status to do with being   educated but they really struggled
at first, financially.   And they wanted to do well.

    They worked very, very hard.   I have some memories
of getting dressed in front of the gas fire,   having a bath
    in front of the gas fire. Having boiled egg and soldiers
on a little table   in front of the gas fire.
        It's taken me a while to realise that it wasn't
everyone's experience. Frugality and   knowing
how to get by on not very much can be very,   very useful.
But I think there's a lot of shame attached to it. Which is
        ridiculous, because there was nothing to be ashamed of.

My mum's dad had some severe mental health issues
        which affected her family…
And they weren't well off anyway.   I think life was probably
quite difficult for her, growing up. There's a lot   of very
English endurance   and kind of stiff upper lip, tough love.
'Get on with it,' and get by on very little.   But then also
a lot of aspiration. And wanting
        to prove that my family is capable of achieving.
    But at the same time, very conflicted.   Because we don't
feel like we deserve it!   I don't deserve to have
    a nice, comfortable time. It's kind of working-class
protestant, I think.   So, yeah.

Publisher

Dear Kate,

I hope your doubts aren't another manifestation of the imposter phenomenon which is jinxing the book…

Eve

I never really planned to be a parent as such –
    well, that's not true, my babies were both planned –
but for a very long time I didn't think
    I was going to have kids, I didn't think I wanted children.

I remember making a bet with a friend
when I was working in Gaza that I wouldn't have babies
before them, and I'd probably never have them.

So when they came along I was sort of unprepared for…
any of it, really. Even though I did the NCT courses,
and I planned the babies…   as I said.

It wasn't the number one thing that I was dreaming about
for my life – becoming a mother.
Which doesn't mean to say that I don't love it
or that I would change it. But I was kind of….

Can you hear the washing machine? OK, that's good.

When the kids came along, I would sometimes just feel
that I was doing a really bad job.   I felt
like everybody around me had planned it for years.
    They'd had this vision of the kind of parenting
they wanted to do, and I was just stumbling along

in the dark.   Sometimes getting it right,
sometimes getting it wrong.

My day job has always been working in education.
    And even though I don't do hands-on teaching
with children, I do quite a lot of work around
play-based learning and inclusion.   So I felt
    like I should know what I was doing.

Just even in a textbook-type way, you know?
    If nothing else.

I wasn't... I didn't have these model kids
    that were clean and tidy and always behaving and doing
exactly what I asked them to do. At the right time.
Eating their food properly at the table.
Not throwing tantrums. All of that.   I just felt
    I was getting it wrong. A lot.

So that really impacted on my life and made me feel crap.
For a long time, I had postnatal anxiety.   And I didn't
identify it properly, for a long time.
And it wasn't until I did identify it – with my GP –
    that I realised that's what was going on. It wasn't
that I was an imposter. It was that I had postnatal anxiety.
    Not postnatal depression, but postnatal anxiety.

And I think the feeling of being an imposter kind of
drove that... If that makes sense?
I didn't even know postnatal anxiety
    was a condition. You know.   It's a bit like the menopause.
Not a health condition we talk about. Because it's
    women's health.

Author

In the beginning, I plan to leave my own, more personal poems out of this book, except the new pieces about historical imposters. I have ideas about publishing the other poems separately, as a pamphlet.

'They're not about imposter feelings,' I say.

'Of course they are,' says the friend who's just read my manuscript. 'They're all about imposter feelings.

It's your book,' she admonishes, 'It's your name on the cover.'

Which is, of course, the problem.

IMPOSTERS (4)

Princess Caraboo (Mary Willcocks)

'She oftentimes carried a gong on her back, which she sounded in a very singular manner, and a tambourine in her hand, the sword by her side and a bow and arrow slung as usual, her head dressed with flowers and feathers, and thus she made it appear she was prepared for war.'

> *Caraboo. A narrative of a singular imposition, practised upon the benevolence of a lady residing in the vicinity of the city of Bristol, by a young woman of the name of Mary Willcocks, alias Baker, alias, Bakerstendht, alias Caraboo, Princess of Javasu.* by J.M. Gutch (1817).

Each morning I dived into in the manor's moss-green lake in only my slick, ottery skin. I swam and flipped, a raving girl again.

I spoke wild, in animal tongues and yips, penned pretty codes on ivory papers, danced in my bare, browned feet. And my gentry hosts – applauded. 'Our esteemed guest from Javasu.' At sundown I prayed to my god from the rooftop the lie might last.

Imagine speaking a language no one understands: that pure music. Little clicks and burrs of my tongue. I never knew so much power in babble, or silence.

Those shapes, those pictograms I scrawled for them on paper: basking cows, a loaded cart on market day, a hatted gentleman, iron window-grid, an arm raised and pleading. They said my hands were soft and showed no sign of wool's scritch or the scrubbing brush, washboard, suds.

At night, I dreamed of Javasu. Did they dream of it too? A sea the deep jade of my newborn's eye, trees loaded with almond-blossom and bulbous fruits, children plump and sleek; temple gongs brassy as wedding bells. The sea's warm lulling, no scalding chill. No sickly, mewling son gone blue, three months since dead in the foundling hospital.

Bloom

After Magda Cordell's 'No. 12'

And I think of all of the times I've emptied
myself – blood-black clots, womb ends,
blossom and stain – into the bowl
or splotched onto white porcelain and tile or
pristine towels, pine boards or intricate
patterned rugs; discarded myself in dark water.

The night gran dies, asleep in a borrowed bed
with my sisters, I soak through
and through everything, sticky and damp
in my aunt's clean sheets. I leak
and spill, terrible, my thighs like steaks,
my womb, my cunt, a pulsing grief.

I think of Marie and the dinner party at her
ex-lover's: white table linen, snow-white linen
covering each high-backed chair; his beautiful,
warm-eyed wife and the silky, melting lamb
in the slow-cooked stew. The wine like
linden blossom, or Mediterranean beach.

The conversation's syncopation, gallant pauses,
kindness. Through the French windows,
Marie watches the garden begin to throb
with crickets in bottle-green dusk. At the end,
when she lifts herself to her feet, her womb
empties its bloody cargo onto the white
in one swift whoosh: bloody rift in the night's
surface. Beautiful, brazen bloom.

Conception

In the fridge, the syringe sits in a cold, serious white box.
It's just past 4am. Fist of belly fat for the needle.

I'm holding my breath. Bee-prick. Mottled peach.
Inside me, the egg follicle swells and blooms,

fleshy and ready to split. My uterus is plush and dark
like an empty carpark slick with rain.

Back to bed. Belly as incubator, loam and meadow.
On the acupuncture couch my muscles have hummed

and levitated, my womb singing with steel and blood.
I've ordered sperm samples from Amsterdam,

submitted to seventeen blood tests, hoicked my legs up
for the fuggy sonar of scans. I've signed to certify

my fitness for parenthood; I've sat on my knuckles
in the counsellor's office, where I spewed

snotty tears, and was pronounced fit for parenthood.
I've made spreadsheets, obsessed, made budgets

and lists, and lists. On the phone from the first clinic (now
abandoned) the receptionist said 'Oh, you're a single –

A single' – She couldn't complete the sentence.
Stalled mid-air at the strangeness. Oh, wordless wonder.

Or incomprehension. Or terror.   I can't turn back.
At the clinic, they jack the bed up to find the right angle

and thread a tube into the dark of me. 'This might feel a bit cold.'
It's that simple. I picture you: an opening out, a crescendo.

RITES/RESOLUTIONS

voices

Olivia

So I try to –
I see ten patients a day   and nine of them are great
and then one gets worse and   'Oh god, that one.'
  But you need to remember the good ones! It's remembering
the positive things that helps. I try to rationalise.
          I try to think

what I would say to a friend.   I remember the good
things I've done.   Or the things that show that I am good
enough…   The things that I have done.

          Because you forget them.
I went through a period of meditating,   but I don't do
that now really. I write in my journal. Not necessarily
positive things, but to get rid of all those negative thoughts,
    clear the brain a bit.

What could people around me do to help? Lots of
reassurance. Just, 'yep you're doing that right.' A little bit of
reassurance goes a long way.   Otherwise you can ruminate.
I used to think that was needy but I think it's not; it's…
knowing that you need…. Support, I guess.
          Time without pressure sometimes. Deadlines are
good but… let me go at my own pace sometimes…

Time, I think. Not being put on the spot maybe.
Having time to prepare.

With the student we had, we were marking her the next day
and meeting to do that. But I, at 10 o'clock the night before,
I was still sitting here with my laptop, writing it all down and
preparing so that I could be really clear   what I was
going to say to her.

I didn't need to do that. But I wanted to prepare.
So I over-prepare.

Not perfectionist but overwork, overachieving. Over-
planner. To get to the same place as everyone else.

I don't know…   I think if your parental figures are not
stable… If you're always trying to make sure they're OK…
You're always trying to fit in aren't you? You're aware
of your not fitting in.

Lolita

When my critic partners first read my book,
they commented on my male characters –
they're soldiers, really, tough boys, they can fight –
all that. But they also have a strong bond
within their team. One of them, at one point, is sad
because his mum is ill.   He doesn't know how
he's going
     to cope. The team leader comes up to him
and gives him a hug, touches his face, tells him
'You're going to be alright,' that kind of thing.

And both my critic partners, who are men, they said
'What's going on here? Are they gay?'
        'No, they're not gay they're just fine with –
emotions, and with admitting there's a problem
and that they need to deal with it.' That assumption:
it tells you a lot about our society.

My parents were the generation after the war.
There was the whole idea that men should provide,
and the woman should be at home. And she's meek

and helpless…   And in families now you get
pulled in two different directions.   The woman
needs to be looking after her family;   the boys
can go out and party.   And at the same time,
the woman   needs to be strong enough to look after
the house and the kids and somehow manage a job
and somehow be – perfect. And we've got this image
    of what is perfect.

And it's just not achievable. To be honest, it's just
    a whole load of bullshit. And it just doesn't make sense.

Why are we putting the bar so high?
On the one hand you're supposed to be independent,
individual, not ask for help – at the same time there's
so much disapproval, so many people telling you
    what you can't do, what's normal.

We need to stop looking at what everyone thinks:
what the neighbours think,   what the family thinks,
what your partner thinks.   I think it has a lot to do with
shame. I see what's happening in America   around
abortion   and it makes my blood boil…

My husband and I –   we could spend all our time
 thinking about what we don't have. We live in a very
materialistic society.   You spend money to make
yourself happy.

But I don't care whether we live in a smaller flat
or a bigger one.   We're healthy, we're happy
with the way our family is, we're trying our best. That's it.

Peter

I wonder how much of it is tied up with the idea that we're
        sold visions of wholeness, constantly…

This is how Capitalism works.   The idea that this
        product, this thing – religion,
self-help approach – will fill the void in your life.

This is the secret.   Here's an image of what life will look
        like when everything's fixed.   And it's serene,
        effortless, graceful. And it's achievable. This person,
        this person in the advert – they've got it.
        They've got it sorted.

It's omnipresent in culture. We are told that there are ways to
        feel qualified, to feel like a non-imposter, to feel real.

If the opposite is entitlement then I think feeling like an
        imposter is healthier overall,   imposter syndrome
        lends itself to a self-reflective sort of character.

I was thinking of rites of passage. There was a programme
        called The Tripods.   I watched it when I was about
        four years old. These beings came from space and
        one of the things
they did was, when you turned eighteen, you'd go through a
        rite of passage where they'd put a thing on your head
that made you really happy and content,   but you wouldn't
        ever think challenging thoughts any more.…

        I still really dislike rites of passage, but I'm increasingly
seeing the value in them.   We're maybe losing them –

these points in your life when you are validated,   somehow
or other   you go through
ceremony, a ritual that actually affirms you
        in a profound way.

    Those times in life when someone says
    'You're part of a community; you're qualified.'

Author

We want to be recognisably ourselves, or most of us
do. At the same time, we're multi-faceted; we contain
multitudes.

I try to think of myself as in process, shifting and
growing rather than static. In her novel *Nights at the
Circus*, Angela Carter describes the city of St Petersburg
as 'built of hubris, imagination and desire... As we are,
ourselves; or, as we ought to be.' If we could all be
fearless enough to view our identities as more mutable
– less life raft, more river or sea – would we still feel
like imposters? I don't know.

Kate

I was talking to my mum about heating,   because it's been
expensive recently, and it's been   very cold recently.
And she said that when she was little, she would go to –
they lived in a house with a coal fire,   one coal fire in the
living-room –

she would go to bed and her dad   would come
to say goodnight, to see her and say goodnight,
and she would say   'Dad I can't sleep, I'm cold,' and he
would say   'Just lie still. You'll get warm eventually.'

I thought, *Wow, that's another era.*   I can't imagine
saying that to my son. I mean, my son is 18 months old, but
   I never want to be saying that to my son.
You know. I might not have central heating, or I might
      not be able to turn it on, but
I'd at least go and get another blanket, if I could. Maybe
   snuggle in together.
      So I think there's a sense that you're not supposed
to complain,   you're supposed to make do.

I worry that if I talk about this to people, they might see it as
kind of whining: *It's not fair. I've got these imposter feelings
holding me back.*   I wanted to talk to people though, find
         a communal way of thinking it through.

I try hard to accept kindness and complements. And to try
to seek out situations where people are supportive. To avoid,
   and to point out, negative stereotypes, lazy stereotypes.
Which is, you know, what I'm trying to do in my teaching –
to be accepting and nurturing. Without making assumptions.

So yeah, I do all the practical things.   Finding perspective,
I think.   I've got a friend who will send – if a job
   comes up she thinks I'd be good at – she'll send it to me.
I really appreciate that. Often, it's the kind of thing where
I've already seen the ad and thought   'Oh no,
      I'd never get that.' So it's really nice that she's thinking
of me like that. So yeah, being recommended for things.
Constructive feedback is lovely, really lovely.

What might make people feel like imposters?

If you feel   you've been lacking some kind of foundation.

I think it can be hard, too, if people around you, or
        people close to you, can't get their head around   what you
do, or your achievements. If it doesn't compute. Maybe
then,   it doesn't compute for you either.

I don't think that feeling inferior and ashamed is the best
        motivation;   I think there are far better motivations.
But I guess imposter feelings have driven me to want
        to teach in a way that makes people feel…
                                as if there are no stupid questions.

I just thought of something and now I've forgotten it. It's
gone, it's gone. It's gone.
            It will come back. No, can't remember. I was just
thinking of…

I was thinking that in some ways my feeling like an imposter
        might be about not wanting   to participate in the
whole social mobility idea.   Not the twentieth century
version of it, anyway. I think it's very damaging
        and unhealthy – the idea   that you should want to sort of
leave behind your origins, socially and culturally.

It's quite messed up.   Obviously, I'm not saying   everyone
should know their place, stick to being   really
            materially deprived.   But yeah.

Do we always need to strive   to leave behind
our supposedly inferior lives, and become something else?

Lynn

What I do to combat imposter feelings? I do tai chi, I do
chi gung, I meditate every day. I do physical exercise.
  I talk to my friends
                (though I should do that more).
I play with my grandchildren. That, in a way,   subsumes
all the negativity. I'm too busy living, intensely – as you do
with children. I read and I write. I try to imbibe
that which is uplifting. To not   allow myself to flail
around in the slough of despondency.   And actually
the other thing, which I wish I employed better, is just to
allow myself to feel those feelings.

Because they're going to dissolve. They're not going to stay.
But you have to allow them
    to dissolve rather than flatten them down. Stay with them.

I've just been reading this little book by Jess Phillips.
You know, the MP.   Imposter syndrome comes up twice.
      I'll just tell you this. If you don't mind,   and you have
time? So she's talking about gaslighting here.   You know,
she talks about where gaslighting comes from: a particular
play in which the husband   manipulates his wife into
      believing that she's imagining the dimming of the lights
in the house, when in reality he's causing it   by turning off
lights in a secretly sealed off attic. She says:
      'Gaslighting is incredibly powerful and relies on existing
hierarchical lines which breed imposter syndrome.'

It's all about power.

Well that's wonderful, yes. It's all about power. And maybe
it is –   but where did you get the idea that others
    are more powerful than you?

Maybe if you start to feel imposter feelings   it's a signal
that in the relationship you're part of,
   or the constellation that you're part of, something is wrong.
It's an alarm signal.

Tiffany

I've done a lot of self-work, increased my self-worth.
My imposter syndrome has been driven down.

I've strived. I've had big ambitions. I have a strong
work ethic. I do want to prove   myself. I want to leave
a legacy, especially for my daughter.

Now, I'm able to look at the facts and listen
   to people. Not   throw a pity party.   I take off
      the shit-tinted spectacles and I look at the evidence. So

      if I've been published I accept that,   even if
         I'm not completely happy with the work.
      If I'm thinking, *Well, you haven't published anything
   in a year –*   *are you still a poet?* I'll stop,
because it's nonsense.

I practise gratitude. I retune my thoughts to be useful and
creative. Self-doubt can be lazy thinking.

I do occasionally think *I'm doing really well.*
   I've got a good network around me.   I've learned
to keep good people close to me.   Being grounded by
people you respect   is one of the best methods for living,
   I find.

         Healthy mental living. Belonging, you know?
it's tribal. But if you look   at some of the great artists

like Van Gogh, and, god, you could pick so many
of them, and....

so many problems, but they created great work.
And probably a lot of them had imposter syndrome but –

they created masterpieces. And whether that came out of
a healthy or an unhealthy place is by the by sometimes but...

We'd rather it were healthy, right? We'd rather
it were healthy.   Would we have the masterpieces
with us today if those artists hadn't been tortured?
I don't know.
        I don't know.

Tabitha

Imposter syndrome's very internal isn't it. You don't have
perspective. You need somebody else to jolt you out of it.

It feels natural to be self-deprecating,   putting yourself
down.   I think what's harder is working out what's
driving it. When I applied for the job and I found I had low
confidence,   I found it really helpful to write down
everything I was worried about –

                actually in a Word document and then pretend to
be somebody else talking back to those worries.   I found
that really helpful. So,

   You don't know anything about this area of prescribing.
   and then, 'No – technically you've got 10 years of
experience.'

What's hard to deal with is that generalised feeling of
I'm not good enough.

For somebody to be able to help,
    they need to know that it's happening.
For a lot of people, they don't feel they can articulate
their imposter feelings, or they don't feel like they're
in a safe enough space to. So if people had a basic level
of awareness that others might be experiencing it and going
through it, what the warning signs might be…

And also – like with people I line-manage –
I think really getting to know them is important.
Because what might seem like a lack of confidence might be,
or might not be.

When I was going for the interview, I spoke to someone
I used to work with who I really rate. She said, 'No you
could do this job, and they'd be lucky to have you.' I didn't
completely believe her, but just hearing it was helpful.

  And you have to be honest; you can't tell someone
something that's not true – that would do more harm than
good. But being authentic, telling someone they're capable.
  It sounds quite basic, but it is that simple sometimes.

If you need anything else Kate just, don't hesitate. Shout.
 Any advice on the research. Just… shout.

Author

Parenthood is, as some of these interviews show, a
fertile space for imposter feelings. For me, though,
growing and giving birth to a new person has meant
grasping and holding something I've wanted for almost
all of my life. Whirling around the living-room singing
along to 'Mamma Mia' with my enthusiastic three-year-
old is, it turns out, a white-hot joy.

Talking to Bill Moyers in 1989, Toni Morrison described parenting as, for her, a kind of liberation: 'Somehow all of the baggage that I had accumulated as a person about what was valuable just fell away. I could not only be me – whatever that was – but somebody actually needed me to be that...'

Here I am, standing – or dancing – in my own body, at the centre of my own life, instead of skulking at the peripheries.

Eve

I think it's important to surround yourself with people who are allies. And supporters. Not to blow smoke up your bum,   but to know you. To remind you why you do it, what brought you there in the first place.

I think that the socially constructed nature of competition and, kind of, capitalism, is what makes people feel like an imposter. I think. That kind of competitive nature,
    survival of the fittest. I feel like that's what drives the psychology that people grow up with.   Or grow into.

I was reading something this morning about immigrant
    populations in the US, that there was a narrative within the family of excellence, and striving for excellence. And deserved excellence. Because, you know,
    their grandfathers' grandfathers
had been enslaved people. And so their time had come.

I dunno,   I just found that quite interesting.
Just, you know, 'Haven't got time for imposter syndrome.'

This was their time.   Maybe they see it as, like,
a construct which has partly been fabricated
        to keep people down.

One of the things I've noticed since moving back to Norwich
is that there's a massive class difference,
        which I never felt in London.
In London, I was surrounded by people who
had pulled themselves up by their education. I felt it was
the educated classes, rather than a class defined
        by economic status.

I met a lot of friends here through baby groups.
We've all had that bonding experience of having babies
        at the same time and now our kids are growing up...

One of the things I have observed with my friends
who come from privileged backgrounds and have
        a public-school education
is their confidence levels are so much higher....
                than anybody who's been brought up in a sort of
working-class or lower middle-class type environment.

That's something that I've observed –
        that there's a complete self-belief and also a sense
of ownership.   Imposter syndrome is not on the agenda
at all... 'Cos there's just a presumption
        that the world is their oyster, it's theirs for the taking.

I feel that really strongly, actually. I feel it more.

It still shocks me now, actually. I went swimming
        the other day at this place
        that was really beautiful. And the woman
who owns the place, runs the place was just sort of,
'Oh my other friend who's got her own estate.'

And you just think *Don't talk to me about estates.*
You know, *I lived on an estate.* D'you know what I mean?
It's a bit shocking,   And it's also realising, you know,
I was in a bubble before, wasn't I? I was in
      my own little echo chamber.

Babies are a leveller, in a way, and then the cracks
      in the fences emerge more profoundly as time goes on.

I think, there's something about....
You know what I said about that lecture, that series of
lectures that I over-prepared for?
Well actually, in a way, that was a good thing, because I did
a bloody good lecture! And that made me feel good
about my job. And myself.

So imposter syndrome can give you, it can, weirdly, give you
a bit of an edge. You know. And it can be quite compelling.
      In a way. That desire to improve.

And for me it's a lot about learning. I really love
learning new stuff. Reading new stuff. I just find it
a complete and utter joy. And if I didn't have that in my life,
I think I would be quite a dull person – I mean,
I don't know what I would do actually, if I didn't
      have that.

I don't know what it is about current parenting culture...
I just used to feel such an imposter.   I used to
beat myself up quite a lot. But I look back now, you know,
      I get those time warps on my phone or whatever.
'You were doing this 4 years ago' – and I just think,
Oh, my kids were great! What was I even worrying about!
I've got lots of pictures of me doing lovely, playful things
and us doing lots of activities together – music, crafts,
            baking, stories...

I just think *gosh, where did that voice come from
that was telling me I wasn't doing anything right?*

Author

Rachel Cusk, writing about Kazuo Ishiguro's novels,
including *Never Let Me Go*, in *The Guardian* in 2011,
accuses him of 'camouflaging the writer's authority
and hence his responsibility'. The particular way
Ishiguro inhabits characters' voices to tell his stories
is, she suggests, 'a type of impersonation'.

'Impersonation,' Cusk argues, 'is also hubris, arrogance,
control, for it seeks to undermine or evade the empathetic
basis of shared experience.'

It strikes me, reading Cusk's article now, after editing
all of my interviews, that this evasion of shared exper-
ience happens when we deliberately pretend to be
someone else – and also when we *feel* we are pretending.
Whatever the reasons behind our imposter feelings, the
nagging sensation of feeling like a fraud gets in the way
of the intimate, empathetic connection that can happen
when we believe we are seen, accepted, and understood.

Sinéad

I value the, the...
                    Something like this project.

I sort of thought   *That's so interesting because
we live with it*. I know lots of people who feel the same way.

And I have felt it. Really strongly, I have felt it physically,
you know. Like when I met up with

those poets in London.   I feel a certain way.
I feel that my voice won't work.   I feel breathless.

I try to see it, feel it, recognise it. Talk to friends
about it, and with my partner. Do things that are a bit scary.

And there might be a bit of reality, like *Actually, I need*
to do some training. That's why I feel so bad. I need

to do an MA in creative writing!   I need to solve
that problem. And then it's just a problem to be solved.

It's not – part of me. The part of me is, you know, the child
who keeps having to go to a new school. OK,

I'll just look after that child and then do the training.

          I have very, very mixed feelings about self-reflection.

Sometimes being bad or in the wrong place is quite positive
or creative. Or just acting on instinct.

Not constantly double thinking oneself. It could be freeing.
          We could all behave better

towards each other and make life easier for each other.
That is very true. Like a campaign to make women not feel

like second-class citizens. That would be good…   I guess
     hierarchies are part of the issue. They thrive

on some people feeling a bit less than, doubting
their abilities and what have you.   I suppose most of our

institutions tend to be quite hierarchical. And we probably
fall into patterns of hierarchy in lots of situations....

So I think we're all conditioned by those unconscious
things. If someone is leader, other people tend to think of

themselves as less than.   Whereas it could just be
that their life lends itself to leading at that time.... I think

I've said it. I keep repeating myself.... But if you've gone
to a certain kind of school you will be in a certain

bracket of achievement.   And if you are white you will have
a certain privilege that people of colour don't so,

you know, it's all set up for people to feel that they have to
place themselves on a scale of...   belonging.

How do people not internalise that, see beyond it,
do what they want anyway? I'd imagine there's a number

of things there which have to do with early childhood
experience, or personality. But they're very

powerful, the...   You know, the social
structures are hard to break. We've changed very slowly.

And it's great when somebody does buck the trend
or whatever. But I guess it's quite useful to a certain section

of society if another section is not competing with it.
Imposter syndrome is quite a useful means of...

social control.   It's really bad, yeah.   I'm not advocating
for it at all!

Well, thank you for the opportunity... Probably don't send me the recording, no. I'd probably... cringe

at the sound of my voice. It's always surprising isn't it, when you see a transcript. You think *Did I say that?*

Oh, it's starting to rain outside. Oh, hurray.

Past Tense

– He said: I'm looking for someone to dance around the kitchen with, to Stevie or James Brown.

– He said: I'm into self-improvement, running, meditation, yoga.

– He said: I'll know her when I see her.

– He said: you don't mind waiting a few minutes, do you?

– He said: are you a night owl? Are you up to much? I'm on the river – we're drinking shots.
   It's hectic.

– He said: can you send a full body photo?

– He said: what's the catch? There has to be a catch.

– He said: can I ask when your last relationship ended, and why?

– He said: where do you see yourself in five years' time?

– He said: I have to finish tidying my desk. I'll be there ASAP.

– He said: the sky's extraordinary tonight. Fifteen, sixteen shades of pink.

– He said: so what happened? Did he get what he wanted and then do the dirty on you?

– He said nothing. Checked his phone, apologised, checked his phone, apologised.

– He said: what are you reading?

– He said: I don't like doing the legwork. I let the ladies come to me.

– He said: I am reading Erich Fromm's *The Art of Loving*.

– He said: can I meet you a little bit later? Later than that? No, later.

– He said: let's play it by ear.

– He said: what are you wearing?

– He said: I'm travelling for work, but I can meet you at the station.

– He said: I've been held up; I'll be there in 20.

– He said nothing. You looked at your icecubes and rattled the glass.

– He said: my friends say I'm a really great catch.

– He said: do you feel anything at all?

Lullaby No. 3

I repeat the word 'sleepy' until my son rubs his paws against his eyes.

I recite all his books from memory, and paint the illustrations
with my voice, and I sing goodnight to the stars and the air, the oak tree
outside our window and that yellow camper van, our laundry rack
and unwashed dishes, porridge smeared up the wall.

And if I diffuse lavender oil into the air,
and rub his chest and legs with warm oils of chamomile and lavender.
If I remember all seventeen steps of our Viennese waltz, and don't blank
                                                        or stumble;

Now I point to the moon, who is sleeping. I say 'Go like that.'
Now I haul him back from his somersaults, his kicking tailspin. I wrestle
                                                        him back
from the top of the stairwell, the window ledge, knife-blade, the heart-
                                                        stopping edge.

If I say 'No, no' to cat's tail-yanking, hair-pulling, hurtling-crescendo, and
                                                        he listens;
If I am calm, and think calm thoughts;
If I see the world in a pastel, picture-book palette, shut out the pelting rain
and the creaking girders, the icy ocean beneath us...

If I am good, deserving of sleep: not a slather-toothed wolf in disguise.
If I bury my anger deep. If I breathe. If I think kind thoughts about those
                                                        that pain me
(may they be happy, may they be well).
If my body is warm, and close at hand. If I count, exhale.
If tomorrow can still be salvaged: patched and pinned with moxy and
                                                        guile...
If I breathe. If I breathe. If my milk is sweet.

After Pretence

I used to confuse desire with a longing
for humiliation; desire as a mean conspiracy
of genitals and hormones. A tongue lapping

hungrily at the dirt, bones worn away
by luminous pleasure. Dust, then nothing.
As a little girl, I read too many books.

I'm pretending the past only matters
as far as I can make use of it; I carry it around
like a set of portable screwdrivers. My body

is a body is a body, fit for the essential functions:
two thirds water, enough heart muscle
to keep me buoyed and afloat. And desire

is a pan of dhal, puttering softly, all day,
at the back of the hob, swelling the kitchen
with musk and yellow sunlight.

.

NOTES

'Introduction: Among the Pretenders' draws on the following texts in particular:

'The Imposter Phenomenon in High-Achieving Women', Pauline Clance and Suzanne Imes, *Psychotherapy: Theory, Research and Practice Volume 15 #3*, 1978.

'Stop Telling Women They Have Imposter Syndrome', Ruchika Tulshyan and Jodi Ann Burey, *Harvard Business Review*, 11 February 2021.

'Am I an Imposter, or Am I Oppressed?' Shivani Seth, *Rest for Resistance* (online), 7 April 2017.

'Why Everyone Feels Like They're Faking It', Leslie Jamison, *The New Yorker*, 6 February 2023.

'Imposter Syndrome as a Public Feeling', Maddie Breeze, *The Sociological Review Magazine* (online), 20 May 2017.

37:    'Imposters' (1) is informed by Kelsey Miller's 'The Real Story of the Fake Anastasia', *Refinery* 29 (online), May 2016.

73:    'Imposters' (2) reproduces text from *The Female Soldier. Or, the Surprising Life and Adventures of Hannah Snell, born in the City of Worcester*, Anonymous, 1750.

75:    'Imposters' (3) borrows small amounts of text from 'Maybe She had So Much Money She Just Lost Track of It' by Jessica Prestler, *The Cut* (online), May 2018.